WRITE ICONIC CHARACTERS

UNLOCKING THE CORE MOTIVATIONS THAT FUEL UNFORGETTABLE STORIES

CLAIRE TAYLOR

FFS MEDIA

Cover Design © FFS Media LLC

ISBN: 978-1-959041-19-1

www.ffs.media

Author photograph by Anna Monette

CONTENTS

THE FEELING CENTER

THE THINKING CENTER

THE ACTION CENTER

BEYOND DOMINANT TYPE

SECTION 4: THE FIRST STEP

INTRODUCTION

THE STRUGGLE OF KNOWING YOUR CHARACTERS

I made it three full books into my series when I realized that I didn't know who the hell my protagonist was. To be clear, I knew which character was the protagonist, but as far as how *deeply* I knew her, it was about on par with a coworker you wave to in the hallway and occasionally crack jokes with at the weekly meetings.

To give myself a little bit of credit, the first three books took place over the course of the protagonist's birth through her high school graduation, so she didn't know who the hell she was, either. But she wasn't the one writing the story. I was. I needed to know who she, Jessica, was (outside of God's only begotten daughter). So, as my protagonist entered her college years, doing all of those things that we tend to do around that age to find ourselves, I was flailing around trying to find her, too.

I feel comfortable offering up this confession to the world because I know how many other authors can relate. You've probably experienced that pause midway through a chapter, the small twitch below the eye, and the question: *Do I even know who this character is?*

There's no correct entry point to a story idea, so authors enter a story inspired by plot, a character, a premise, an idea (or something else) … and then we hit the page. Maybe you had a solid premise, like I did, and then dove in without knowing much about it because it was NaNoWriMo time and you had to get to typing. Maybe you saw a particular scene unfolding and your mind wondered how someone would find themselves in that position, and that's what drew you to the idea.

There are a million different creative lures that hook into our imagination and drag us into the novel, so it's incredibly common to overlook something that seems as obvious, in retrospect, as who your protagonist is on a fundamental human level.

Or non-human, depending on the genre.

Thankfully I had some tools at my disposal for figuring out who Jessica was, beyond who her father happened to be. There was the whole creative writing degree thing, sure, but let's be honest about how easy it is to get through four years of *that* without learning some basic skills. I was a straight-A student and graduated with the ability to talk at length about the symbolism of orangutans in Poe, but couldn't with any confidence define the term "theme."

My degree was not the tool that I fell back on to figure out how to go deeper in my exploration of Jessica. Instead, as I was fighting a losing battle with the start of the fourth book of the series, I turned to this other tool called the Enneagram. I'd heard about it years before from my mom and my sister, who learned about it at their church. Not being involved with religion myself, I'd pretty much written it off as a Jesus-y Myers-Briggs. What they'd taught me about the Enneagram was simple: each type had a number associated with it, and that number, if wielded by someone pure of heart, could be used to adequately shame and belittle others. "You're such a Four, Claire." (I don't actually remember what they thought I was, only that when they described it, it didn't sound at all like me. I'm a pretty typical One.)

In short, I was not a fan at first. It wasn't until years later when my friend Alyssa Archer, who edits all of these Enneagram books for me (and generally keeps me from making an ass of myself in all she edits), convinced everyone in our small author mastermind group to look into the Enneagram.

Growing up in Texas, I'd developed a solid ability to spot covert attempts at religious conversion (accidentally getting "saved" not once but twice in my youth helped fine-tune that). Alyssa didn't ping on my radar as that type, so I gave this Enneagram thing a shot and took a test online that told me that I was either a Three or a One.

I read up on the Three, which was called the Achiever, and thought, *Yeah, that sounds a little bit like me.* High achievement, always trying to hit goals, sure. But then I read up on the One, called the Reformer, and the soul-level cringing began. Perfectionist? Yep. Always feeling compelled to do the right thing even if it derails your plans? Yikes. Unreasonably high standards of quality beyond the point that anyone else would notice, let alone care? *Oof*.

As the description went on, I started to think there might be something to this whole Enneagram thing. The Myers-Briggs, DISC, the Big 5, and all those other personality frameworks held a mild interest for me, insofar as it's sometimes fun to slap the label on like a badge when someone brings it up in conversation, but reading about my Enneagram type felt like someone had hacked into my operating code. And the code wasn't all that flattering. Not to mention discovering all of the malware in there that I hadn't addressed.

While I did find myself cringing, one thing I didn't find myself doing was looking away. I couldn't. I was seeing parts of myself that were true, and more than that, I was seeing that the parts of myself that were making me miserable were things that could change. It was painful but also hopeful.

At its core, the Enneagram is a measurement of internal motivation. It breaks down nine core fear and core desire pairings that drive human behavior. This will probably activate something in your writer mind—motivation is an essential thing to know about our characters if we want to move them physically, emotionally, and intellectually. When we know what a character's core motivation is, we become puppet masters in a way where the strings aren't getting all tangled and we know how to move the sticks to get the marionettes to do exactly what we want.

All that thinking, feeling, and behaving in our characters starts with a core fear and core desire of the Enneagram type. So, as I sent Jessica off to college in book four to experiment and discover who she was, I dug in and decided on her Enneagram type, based on the patterns I'd written into her for the first eighteen years of her life. I analyzed how she made her decisions, what emotional patterns she followed, and the terms in which she saw the world. There were a few top candidates for types, as there usually are when we're looking at children and teens, but ultimately there was a winner.

Surprise, surprise. She was a One, just like me.

To some subconscious extent, I'd been writing her this way the whole time. When I put her in a tough situation, I'd ask: *What I would do in that situation?* Then I'd have her do, think, or feel something similar.

This accidental type syncing is incredibly common for authors who don't know the Enneagram. Before learning about the Enneagram, and beginning to understand the deep distinctions between types, it's easy to project our own core motivations onto a character. The result, especially when writing a character of a very different type, can be a muddled mess. We may instinctively know that their motivations aren't the same, yet we project our own onto them in crucial points of the plot. Savvy readers will sense the inconsistency and exclaim, "This character wouldn't do that!" And they're probably right.

This isn't because all of our readers are Enneagram experts, but because as humans we're intuitively familiar with each type's common patterns. After all, we've met them in our lives or in the books that we read over and over again.

The Enneagram framework helps us recognize and describe

patterns that naturally exist in human psychology, but without knowing the language of it, it's easy to get off track.

Once it became firm in my mind that Jessica was an Enneagram Type 1, frequently called the Reformer, her character made so much more sense to me, and I wasn't surprised that I had made the reluctant daughter of God a Reformer and plopped her down in the middle of West Texas to face all kinds of dogma and misogyny that just didn't seem right to either her or me. In fact, it made total sense that I, a Reformer myself, would come up with this idea and like it enough to see it through seven books.

I won't say that books four through seven were easy to write (sweet baby Jessica, they were a pain in the ass), but I will say they were certainly made slightly easier by knowing who Jessica was. She found herself, and I found her, in those college years. It invited me to love her more, brought us closer together, and made it so much easier for me to torture her in just the right way, which I did pretty much nonstop until the final page of the series.

This was a turning point in my writing career. In the next series I started after using the Enneagram for Jessica Christ, I knew the protagonist's type from the get-go, which helped me know how to motivate her. (She was a psychic sleuth, so I needed to know exactly how to motivate her to get involved each time someone croaked, even if it was none of her business.) I also knew what her gifts were and what she brought to the world that was desperately needed, as well as how people could use her weaknesses against her.

That's still my bestselling series to date, and I credit my protagonist with most of that success. People had to care about her to want to read thirteen mysteries with her at the center. But first *I* had to care about her. Before you can deeply love someone, you have to deeply know them. The Enneagram is the best way I have found, and I've searched a lot of corners of humanity to learn how best to love others.

The more you love your characters as their creator, the more iconic they'll become. But first, you must understand them, not just your protagonist but also your secondary characters, and even (or especially) your villains.

You don't have to become an Enneagram expert to discover its usefulness in writing characters. While much of my depth of knowledge now is a result of learning from experts in the field through training and certification processes, even more of it was gained from application. Even prior to any formal training, I was able to dive in and find great usefulness in the framework, and I'm certain you'll be able to do the same.

The Enneagram is a tool you can use to go as deep as you want or stay as surface-level as you want while still reaping rewards. There's really no end to the depth of learning available to you, but what I hope to do in this book is offer you enough to get started.

Being able to describe these nine distinct types is complicated work, though, and it involved intentional learning so that I could effectively deploy the Enneagram's helpful framework in all of my important characters. As writers, it's right in our wheelhouse to use words to describe things, so that's what this book is about: how to do that with the Enneagram.

That protagonist you can't figure out yet, that villain that's not as interesting as you'd hoped—by the end of reading this book I want you to hold the key to unlocking that character so that you can dive back into writing more enthusiastically and confidently than before.

And don't worry if you're already a few books into your series before you start doing this character work. Readers have stuck with you so far, and making the characters they already love stronger and more fleshed out is only going to make the reader love them more. If you want to go back and do some rewrites on previous books in the series to align your characters to a type more strongly, that's okay, too.

Personally, that sounds like hell on earth to me, and it's often not worth the effort insofar as increasing sales goes. We get to make a lot of mistakes as authors without readers catching on. Improving our craft is a natural process that doesn't require hating everything we've done before (or rewriting it). Going from good to great doesn't mean that what was once good is now bad. Take it from me, a recovering perfectionist and forever a Reformer.

WHY AM I THE GAL FOR THE JOB?

Nothing kicks up my sassiness more than someone asking me why I was the right person to write a particular book. Yes, I've had people ask me this question before. Weird, right? It takes everything in my power not to say, "Because I'm the person who sat her ass in the chair and wrote the damn thing," or even snarkier, "What qualifications do you think I might be missing?"

When it comes to a topic like this one, though, I do think it helps you, the reader, to settle into the material knowing that you're in good hands. I certainly don't know everything on this topic, and I'm learning more every day, so while I might be considered an expert by some, I also consider myself to be a dedicated student when it comes to the Enneagram in general and how it relates to storytelling in specific.

As for the official-sounding stuff, I'm an Advanced Certified Instructor of the Enneagram Spectrum of Personality Styles, having studied under Jerome Wagner, PhD. I'm also recognized by the Integrative Enneagram as an Accredited Practitioner, having completed their requirements for certification for both individual and teams coaching.

On top of that, I've been studying the Enneagram on my own for almost a decade, using it to write fiction in the genres of satire, sci-fi, crime fiction, and paranormal cozy mystery as well as shaping my career to align with my internal motivation.

I've consulted with hundreds of authors individually on their books and series and presented Enneagram material and hosted workshops and masterclasses to thousands of authors across the industry, from small virtual writing groups to big stages.

I've coached hobby writers and *New York Times* bestsellers, unknowns and breakout sensations, young parents and new widows. The stories I hear are each unique and yet all are familiar and deeply human.

If there's a genre that I haven't coached yet, I simply haven't heard of it. Sweet rom-coms, gritty cyberpunk, reverse harem, paranormal sapphic romance, cozy horror—you name it, and I've had the absolute pleasure of playing around in the sandbox with one of those authors.

The genres look different, sure, but the deep motivations of the characters are universal in the same way that the Enneagram is universal while containing so much diversity.

The work that has gone into creating and refining the Enneagram with all its types, subtypes, vices, vulnerabilities, virtues, core wounds, idealized self-image, and so forth is a tremendous effort that includes contributions from brilliant minds, powerful hearts, and attuned bodies of psychotherapists, social workers, and spiritual leaders of every major religion and spiritual practice. And the development is ongoing. I think that's what I love the most about the Enneagram—it allows for deeper and deeper discovery, which means that it can contain the nuances of each of us. It's a framework, a road map of how we function, through which we can locate ourselves and begin to ask if there are other ways we'd like to exist in this world and if some of the patterns that we thought were helping us have actually been limiting us in unseen ways.

While I doubt we will ever see a new type emerge, turning the Enneagram into the Decagram, I do view it as a tool for discovery just as much as a tool for learning what's already been discovered. I enjoy reading nonfiction broadly, and after devouring books on psychology, sociology, personality, spirituality, consciousness, and the so-called supernatural, I have yet to find *anything* that breaks the model of the Enneagram. It all seems to layer on top of it quite nicely. And yes, I have been probing myself for confirmation bias.

I consider myself an Enneagram skeptic. That might surprise you to hear, until you realize that one of my big life goals is to never end up in a cult. Just the term

"Enneagram" itself and the shape of the thing sets off my skeptic's radar. I'm not saying that the Enneagram couldn't be misused and distorted for the purposes of a cult, because anything can if you have the right man for the job, but I am saying that there's always a voice in the back of my head going, "Hey, are you sure you're not falling down a rabbit hole that leads to a high-control group?"

I won't say that I've arrived at total certainty about the Enneagram not being the gateway to a cult, but that's only because I've learned that total certainty about anything is a trap. However, I will say that one of the fundamental principles of the Enneagram is that it shows each of us how to achieve *liberation*. No obedience to an external authority required or desired.

The Enneagram is a map that each of us can learn to read independently. It doesn't require any sort of guru to interpret it for us, though I would be remiss if I didn't mention that coaching can be extremely helpful when it comes to seeing what we're not seeing about ourselves. But the Enneagram and all the shared learning about it allows us to explore on our own time and draw our own meaning from it.

In fact, that's the whole point of the Enneagram—not to put us in a box, but to liberate us from the box we've constructed around ourselves to keep us safe. It frees us from patterns of thinking, feeling, and behaving that disconnect us from our deeper nature and therefore limit our ability to connect to others and the world around us.

This liberation comes through a process of learning to understand our core fear and begin to observe our thoughts, our feelings, and our physical sensations without letting them rule us. It liberates us, or frees us, to make the best decisions for our ability to give and receive love and to live mindfully in this world, moving closer to truth rather than shying away from it.

This process of liberating myself from my fear has done pretty incredible things for me, but because I recognize that I have a tendency to preach, I'll just leave it at that for now.

My first two nonfiction books, *Reclaim Your Author Career* and *Sustain Your Author Career*, were designed to help authors find their feet, align their writing life to their motivation, and build a career that won't crumble from the industry's constant shifting beneath their feet. If you're interested in using the Enneagram for your own career and well-being, go check out those books.

This book, however, isn't all about you. Phew, right? Examining your deepest self can be exhausting and downright shitty work sometimes, and authors I'm coaching frequently try to steer the subject away from themselves by asking how to use the Enneagram for their characters. I get it. This is the fun part.

So, finally, *finally*, I'm taking the time to dive fully into this topic. Honestly, jailbreaking all the information I've been holding in my head about each type and how to use it specifically for creating excellent, and dare I say *iconic*, characters is so much fun that my Type 1 almost doesn't consider it work. (I'm sure I'll find a way to make it feel high stakes enough that it becomes less fun, don't worry.)

I'm the gal for the job when it comes to writing this book because I've been applying what I've learned for years, I know how much author suffering I can alleviate by sharing my acquired knowledge with the world in book form (hello, it's a LOT), and because, dammit, I'm the gal that's sitting her ass down in the chair and writing it.

At this point, you couldn't stop me from writing this book if you tried. (And I know that because you're reading it, so it's already published. Ha! Good luck inventing a time machine!)

If I'm the gal made to write this book, then you're the (gender-neutral) gal made to read it. I hope my boring-ass résumé and personal experience gives you the peace of mind to sit back and believe me when I say it'll be worth your time.

WHAT IS AN ICONIC CHARACTER?

An iconic character is one who sticks with us long after we've finished enjoying the story. They become a personal reference point, the kind of figure we might use to describe our friends … or our enemies.

These characters strike at something fundamental to the human condition, even if they aren't *strictly* human. They take on a life of their own, to the point where we, as readers, might know exactly what that character would say in a particular situation. We may even hear their voice in our head, even if we've only ever read their words. When we encounter an iconic character, they become a part of our psyche.

As an author, striving to write at least one iconic character is the best thing you can do for your career. So many other small mistakes we make as writers can be forgiven if the characters strike deep to our readers' humanity, whether that's connecting with their better nature or their shadow self.

To understand the process of crafting these sorts of icons, we must learn some basics about the human psyche, and this book is designed to do just that. I'll be breaking down the nine core fears and desires that live inside each of us to varying degrees. These fears and desires motivate every choice your iconic character must make, right down to the formation of their thoughts, feelings, and actions.

The rest of this book is designed to help you master these skills so you can write characters whose stories readers simply cannot put down.

SECTION 1: THE ENNEAGRAM

A MOTIVATIONAL FRAMEWORK

WHAT IS THE ENNEAGRAM?

Allow me to clear my throat and straighten my tie as I get somewhat technical and theoretical in this section. I touched on this before, but I think it's incredibly useful to understand *why* the Enneagram works as well as it does as a framework for understanding people and therefore characters. As a One (you'll learn more about this type in Section 3), I do have a tendency to argue my case like a lawyer, so I'll try not to beat you over the head with my evidence. *Your honor, I think it's clear that the Enneagram is a tool that all authors would benefit from learning, and throughout these pages I'll prove that case beyond a reasonable doubt.*

The Enneagram is a tool that shows us how each of the nine types' core motivations influence its 1) thoughts, 2) feelings, and 3) behaviors. It is a psychological framework that shows us how our underlying fears manipulate our attention, shape the way we think, provoke our strongest feelings, and direct our actions in ways that we are not necessarily aware of.

3

The core fear and core desire that make up the "motivation" for each type are two sides of the same coin. For instance, Type 5, commonly called "the Investigator," has the core fear of being incompetent or incapable and the core desire of being competent and capable. The desire is essentially to *not experience the fear*, and the fear is that you will *not fulfill the desire*. For this reason, it can often be easiest to simply focus on remembering the core fear associated with each type to keep it simple. Fear resonates with us on a primal level and can be easier to relate to, anyway.

These nine Enneagram core fears are not of things like spiders or heights—any of the types can pick up those fears separately—but rather, they're *social* fears. For social animals, social fears are just as potent and dysregulating as physical danger, sometimes more so, to the point where a person might risk bodily harm to avoid their fear of, say, being controlled by others (think: fighting against an unjust power).

To drive this point home, let's take the iconic character of Indiana Jones. His most obvious fear, the one we all know about, is snakes. "Snakes" is not one of the core fears of the Enneagram, though. So, what is his core fear? I would argue his core fear is actually that of the Seven, sometimes called "the Enthusiast," which is to be trapped in pain and deprivation. The man was an archaeology professor who took just about any excuse to ditch the classroom for adventure, and if there was a fine new broad for him to flirt with, even better. He wasn't fighting off Nazis so much as he was fighting off boredom, is what I'm saying. Anyone reading this who's a Seven will know exactly what I mean, because they were likely chided by their teachers growing up for not staying in their seat and focusing on the task at hand. It's not a lack of intelligence that leads to their seemingly short attention span; it's the fear of deprivation in a world full of possibilities. Restlessness is a strong visceral experience for the Seven.

It's important to acknowledge that none of the nine core fears will sound appealing to *anyone*. You're unlikely to hear someone beg to be trapped in pain and deprivation (the fear of the Seven) outside of, perhaps, a dark romance, and even then, it's mostly consensual. However, for each person and character, *one* of the core fears will inevitably be the *most* intolerable. The type with the most intolerable fear to a person is what we call that person's "dominant type." Almost all of our default thoughts, feelings, and actions are developed at a young age to help us avoid this core fear.

Mostly, these are lines of code running in the background of our mind that we're not even aware of. This expression of type could take the form of an emotional pattern of envy, a thinking pattern of worry, or a behavioral pattern of recklessness, for instance. These patterns of thinking, feeling, and doing that we repeat become the armor that we wear to protect us from that thing we fear most as we survive in a chaotic world.

Some people call this armor "personality," and some call it our ego. It's not uncommon for someone to feel like that's all they are, a collection of their patterns of thinking, feeling, and behaving, and that if they stop mindlessly following those patterns and choose something else, they won't know who they are. We often tether our identity to these patterns as a way to feel certain in an uncertain world. Altering them in any way, regardless of how maladaptive they've become, can feel like an existential threat. That's how ingrained these patterns become in us.

But they are not us, and that's really good news because it means that we and our characters can let them go when those thoughts, feelings, and actions are not doing the things that we hoped they'd do. We can try something else; we can change. But before we can do that, we have to be able to identify those patterns, to name them. This is a process of self-awareness, and not everyone has the courage or knowledge necessary to practice this process of self-awareness at any given moment. The lack of it leads to most of the suffering in our lives.

Our Enneagram type runs deep. It's often described as a lens because we filter all of our lived experience through it. As a result, people with different Enneagram types can experience the same event and have vastly different takeaways. David Daniels, MD, and Virginia Price, PhD, call this *the perceptual filter*.

The perceptual filter determines what information is relevant in our lives. What we deem to be a threat is considered *highly* relevant, so you might already be able to see how the core fear starts to shape what information our attention shifts toward and what information might be dismissed due to being "irrelevant."

If we're not mindful about it, this perceptual filter could dismiss all the information that isn't relevant to our unexamined core fear, leaving us *only* with information relevant to it. That collection of information shapes our worldview, so if we're unaware that it's incomplete and sorted according to what we perceive as a threat, we may start to believe that threats are everywhere. That makes it difficult to do things like relax, connect with others, experience joy, and all those other things that happen outside of vigilance.

We're all storytellers here, so let me paint you a picture with some words: Imagine you're walking through the woods. You're not lost in the wilderness (scary); you're taking a stroll through a local greenbelt (promising). The weather is just a little on the cool side for you, so that once you start exerting yourself, it'll be just right and you'll stop noticing it altogether. It's sunny, but the forest canopy spares you the harshness of the rays. There's a light breeze blowing through the trail, dancing over your skin and conducting a symphony through the trees.

Within that environment, one that most would consider rather peaceful and uneventful, there's already too much raw information for your brain to absorb and retain all at once. Thankfully, your brain is able to sort by relevancy using that perceptual filter.

What about this environment is most relevant to you? What prickles your fear and what tugs at your desire?

If you have a massive fear of snakes, and that's what you've come to associate the wilderness with, then your attention might naturally be drawn to any bit of brush or piles of rocks where a snake might be hiding. You might naturally be scanning the ground for snakes without even realizing it. Or maybe you do realize it. Maybe you're wishing you hadn't taken this damn hike to begin with because it's not worth managing that fear of snakes. You struggle to relax because you're on high alert for snakes.

Your friend, who's come out on the trail with you, is an avid bird-watcher. They're not particularly hung up on the whole snake thing, because they read at one point that snakes can feel the vibrations of high-traffic paths and generally stay away for their own safety. Because nature doesn't trigger any of your friend's strong fears, the most relevant thing to their attention is their desire to locate birds. Their attention focuses on sounds around them in the hopes of hearing an interesting birdcall that will help them visually locate the bird. As you're scanning the ground, your eyes darting from one potential snake spot to the next, your friend's gaze is aimed up at the trees. They may even be filtering out the sound of your grumbles because it's not relevant to finding birds.

After an hour of this hike with your friend, you emerge from the greenbelt and return to the parking lot. The pair of you have had two vastly different experiences during your time in the woods. You walked the same trails, passed the same trees, saw the same dogs and hikers coming from the opposite direction, yet you would each tell a completely different story about your time on the trail.

If you actually saw a snake on your walk, then the lesson you take away might be that it's not worth going on hikes in the woods because you constantly have to keep an eye out for snakes. If you *didn't* see a snake, your lesson might be something like, *These walks will be more pleasant if I can let myself relax.* Or, admittedly, it could be something like, *I didn't see any snakes, but that might only mean they hide in plain sight better than I thought.*

Meanwhile, your birder friend may leave the woods thinking, *Wow, I need to do this more often.* Or maybe they didn't see a whole lot of birds in the trees and leave thinking, *I need to find somewhere else to hike that's going to yield more bird sightings.*

Either way, when the two of you meet up with a third friend for brunch, your tale will likely involve snakes and your friend's will be about birds because that's where each of your attentional patterns flowed, creating an experience particular to you.

Now, multiply this filtered experience over and over again so that your whole life is walking through the woods. It's going to be hard for you to understand what the bird-watcher is talking about half the time. Their takeaways from experiences are going to seem bonkers to you. "Why do you only ever talk about the trees? You're gonna get yourself killed if you don't occasionally look at the ground for snakes!"

Enneagram lenses work a little like this, except instead of a fear of snakes, which we already established isn't a core fear, a person might have a fear of being harmed and controlled that draws their attention toward any possible traps that could lead to them being harmed or controlled, any metaphorical brush piles where the rare Harm and Control Viper may be hiding. Meanwhile, the birder friend's core fear might be to lack worth and value, so they've learned to look for the colorful Worth and Value Sparrows in the trees that they can brag about finding later.

You might say to your friend, "Hey, I don't think you wanna make that decision because the Harm and Control Viper will bite you if you do," and their response might be, "What are you going on about? Never mind. Hush. I'm trying to find the Worth and Value Sparrow." They don't give much attention to your fear, because they are more concerned with avoiding their own fear and seeking their desire.

I'm certain we've all experienced this with a good friend before. Maybe you consider yourself highly ambitious and you appreciate that about your friend Kelly as well. The two of you work long hours each week that most people would consider grueling or insane. It makes you feel less alone knowing that on those late nights where you're working, Kelly is also working and you can reach out to her and commiserate a little if needed. It may be that ninety percent of the time you and Kelly agree on strategy and industry things.

And then suddenly Kelly voices an opinion that you find so incredibly wrong that it stops you in your tracks and you gag on your own spit. It makes you question your entire friendship with Kelly. Maybe it's advice she gives you on your career that seems so off you wonder if she's trying to sabotage you. Or maybe it's something that's so unethical you wonder if she's been a psychopath hiding in plain sight this whole time. Or maybe she's just said something that sounds so self-defeating you can't continue being her friend without her dragging you down.

This kind of moment happens *all of the time* in relationships. It's usually the result of an Enneagram lens mismatch. You share a strong commonality with someone—a bond that's been holding you together all these years, usually a trait like ambition or determination that a few different Enneagram types tend to exhibit strongly. The result is that you've been walking the path next to your comrade and at the same speed for a while. You've become used to it. You assume that your history of agreeing with each other is a result of you seeing the world in much the same way.

And then you hit a new kind of fork in the road, and you each want to go a different route from the other. Not only that, you're both absolutely certain your route is the correct one.

Learning about Enneagram types is the greatest tool I've found for navigating a situation like this because you begin to realize that you're essentially in the previous scenario about the hike, and your friend has suggested the two of you trek down Deadly Rattlesnake Pass ("Are you out of your fucking mind???") not because they want you to experience the most fear you've ever experienced, but because Deadly Rattlesnake Pass happens to lead to Birder's Utopia.

WHAT WE LOOK FOR, WE ARE LIKELY TO FIND.

When I was younger, I was obsessed with this specific shade of teal that was on a lot of trucks. This was the '90s and, as you may remember, teal was a big fucking deal back then. For whatever reason, I became fixated on cars painted that particular teal. I'd find a vehicle with that hue on it roughly once a day. Sometimes I would point out to people, "Man, there are so many teal trucks in Austin," and they would sort of shrug and go, "I guess so." They weren't looking for that truck. But I was, and the city felt full of them.

When I was younger, I also had this one close friend who told me about the many times she'd been betrayed by her best friends. I thought, *Man, that's some real bad luck. I'll be sure not to betray her.*

What I didn't understand at the time was that she already believed the world was full of best friends who betray you. So it's perhaps not shocking that she eventually accused me of betraying her. I certainly didn't feel like I had done anything that would warrant the label of betrayal, although maybe I'd fallen down on the job of best friend in some small way. Maybe I'd put my own interests ahead of hers when I had to choose between the two. I honestly don't remember the specifics, but I do remember being confused at the accusation of betrayal.

I'm not trying to paint myself as innocent here, because again I don't remember the full details (and kids do shitty things to each other, so I don't have any problem admitting that I was not exempt from that as a child).

Looking back, though, I suspect that she had a keen eye for anything that even so much as hinted at possible betrayal and had, as a result, unintentionally developed a worldview where everyone betrayed her. She couldn't see the times that people didn't betray her when there was an opportunity to do so; she couldn't see the loyalty. Expecting encounter the Betrayal Snake on her hike, she focused all her attention on piles of brush until she found one.

We all do this whether we recognize it or not. When we are unaware of our core fear and how that causes our attention to flow, we don't recognize that we're seeing the world through a filter and not getting the whole picture. But we extrapolate meaning from that incomplete picture all the same. We develop simple creeds that we live by, like "Nobody is coming to save me," or "I'm only as valuable as the people I help."

Since we're able to witness only a small portion of reality, these creeds may be applicable in a small portion of the situations we encounter, but they aren't universal.

That creed of "Nobody is coming to save me," while perhaps true from time to time, may eventually cause us to overlook the people who *are* trying to help us out by throwing us a lifeline. It may keep us from asking for help when help is the only way to accomplish what we truly want to create. As a result of clinging tightly to that creed, we may end up in more and more situations where it would be really nice if someone came to save us, but we overlook everyone's attempt to do so, only reinforcing the creed in our minds and hearts.

This is why the Enneagram is so crucial to understanding human behavior. Not only is it important for each of us reading this book, but as authors, the greatest thing we can do to write iconic characters is to understand human psychology and how people manage to get themselves into and out of major messes.

SECTION 2: THE ENNEAGRAM AND STORYTELLING

STORIES ARE ABOUT PEOPLE

The stories that stick with us forever are, by and large, about people. They're about people experiencing life in ways that are mostly familiar but a little bit novel. Sometimes these people aren't human. Sometimes they're aliens or animals or even old trees. It actually doesn't matter, because it's always humans who are telling these stories, and with very few exceptions, humans are limited to speaking through a human perspective. We project our human perspective onto places where it doesn't belong as a matter of daily life. This impulse itself is sometimes an element of the stories we tell. Maybe it's an AI girlfriend like in the movie *Her*, or a beach ball named Wilson as we see in *Cast Away*. I have a southern live oak outside my office window that I just *know* disapproves of me if I go too many days in a row without meditating.

Even simple stories shared between friends tend to be centered around people. I'm not just referring to office gossip, I'm also talking about that story of the person cutting you off in traffic, or the glorious sunset you witnessed in the grocery store parking lot. In the latter case more specifically, that story was about you. Even though from your perspective you are telling a story about an inanimate object, the sun, interacting with another inanimate object, the Earth, the story itself was about a person and how that natural phenomenon made them (you) feel.

Even "high-concept stories" are not actually about the concept but rather about the characters interacting with that particular concept. The Hunger Games trilogy isn't interesting because of the (somewhat) novel concept of the life-or-death competition. That's a solid hook to bring in readers, sure, but why that hook works is because potential readers are left wondering, *What would a person do in that situation?* And then the trilogy explores that. It explores the characters, the people. *What will she do now?* is the reason why people turn the page. Caring about the iconic characters is what keeps people hooked.

You can razzle-dazzle all you want with the story concept, the setting, and the premise. But if you want readers to stick around, you need to focus on building memorable characters.

Stories are about people, and so the best thing we can do for our storytelling chops is to better understand people.

UNDERSTANDING PSYCHOLOGY HELPS US UNDERSTAND CHARACTERS

I'm sure you're starting to see how understanding human psychology can be massively beneficial to writing iconic characters that feel real and simply resonate with people on a fundamental level. Thankfully, though, we don't have to have a degree in psychology to write fleshed-out and compelling characters.

The Enneagram does much of the heavy lifting for us, as amateur psychologists, once we get the basics under our belt and have the handy resources at our fingertips. It's also why the Enneagram is catching on so rapidly within the storyteller community. Every day, more and more authors refer to the types to guide their character development, and even massive movie studios use the Enneagram for story development. You know those animated movies that rip open your cold, adult heart? Yeah, word on the street is that those writers are using the Enneagram.

Obviously, there are plenty of writers who crafted iconic characters without knowing the language of the Enneagram, and that's because much of it is intuitive. Some people simply have a gift for understanding motivation and knowing what that motivation might lead to or not lead to. They know a type so well that it's second nature for them to write that type. In general, it's their own type placed in an exciting or high-stakes environment or situation.

The issues arise, though, when they try to write characters of another type that they don't know so intuitively. They may get close, but those characters just don't hit quite the same. We see this frequently when authors try to create a spin-off series with a beloved secondary character. The author may be able to grasp the surface-level traits of the secondary character, which is often all they need to create a beloved sidekick or townsperson, but when it comes time to dig into them in depth as a protagonist, the train can't seem to stay on the tracks.

Very few people have the gift of intuitively understanding the common cognitive, emotional, and behavioral schemas of even one core fear. The greatest writers throughout time were experts of the human mind. They studied it and generally were not scared of it, though they warned against certain traps and pitfalls. One way or another, authors who write the characters that resonate with us and stick in our memory are students of psychology, whether they studied it formally or not.

Regardless of how *you* may have studied it, learning about the nine types of Enneagram will organize the information you already know on an intuitive level so that your mind can easily pull what it needs the next time you're wondering what one of your characters would likely do in a given situation.

IMPORTANT ELEMENTS OF THE ENNEAGRAM FOR CHARACTER DEVELOPMENT

People grow. People change. Your characters will hopefully do the same. A character who learns nothing quickly becomes annoying to readers. So, what does that mean when it comes to Enneagram types? Do characters change type over the course of their arc?

Fortunately, no, they do not. That would make this incredibly tricky business.

The Enneagram community has plenty of nitpicky disagreements on how this or that operates, but one thing that is agreed upon is that the *dominant type* (reminder: this is what is colloquially called a person's "type") of a person never changes.

That doesn't mean that the person never changes. That doesn't mean that internal character arcs don't exist in real life.

While maintaining the same dominant type, there are still plenty of possibilities for movement in your character, for change, growth, and (an author's favorite) spiraling. Nothing needs to stay stagnant here.

So, let's talk about these common movements we see, these little weaves and bobs of personality that happen when the situation shifts and the patterns that worked okay for us stop being as effective in the outcome they produce.

There are three main kinds of movement I suggest you look for when writing your characters: Levels of Development, wings, and stress. Understanding how these concepts move (i.e., motivate) your character beyond the standard patterns of their dominant type will help you understand why your gut might be telling you to write something that doesn't strictly stay within a particular type's lane.

Let's look at how each of these works.

LEVELS OF DEVELOPMENT

Each type has nine Levels of Development within it. Levels 1 to 3 are considered "healthy" or "high integration." Levels 4 to 6 are considered "average" or "moderate integration," and levels 7 to 9 are considered "unhealthy" or "low integration." I find that calling them healthy, average, and unhealthy is the easiest for me to remember and grasp, even if one could argue that it attaches a slight stigma to the lower levels.

Personally, I don't mind the idea of a stigma surrounding the "unhealthy" Levels of Development because they are destructive to one's self and others, so, like, maybe we should avoid going there unless we want to be a villain. And if you're intentionally writing a villain, these levels are gold!

We move up and down the levels of our type throughout our life, even throughout our day, as internal and external factors change. Hungry? You might move down a level. Your annoying neighbor left you a passive-aggressive note? You might move down a couple of levels. Did someone show you compassion when you expected to be berated? You might move up a level or two there.

For the purpose of writing a character, it's useful to understand that all the levels aren't available at any given moment. We have what Riso and Hudson describe as a "center of gravity" that lands around one of the levels. For instance, your hero's center of gravity might be at level 4. That's where they spend the most time. However, they have "bandwidth" of a few levels, which means they may have access to levels 3 and 2, and then may occasionally sink down to levels 5 and 6. Maybe they stretch up to level 1 here and there. Maybe they even sink down to level 7. But mostly they'll hover around level 4 and probably not sink down to level 9 without you giving them a serious villain origin story.

Meanwhile, your villain's "center of gravity" is likely lower in the levels, and they probably won't have access to levels 1 to 3 within their "bandwidth."

Most of us, and most of our characters, will spend most of the time in the average levels (levels 4 to 6). These levels are where personality really personalities. The patterns are loud and proud. We're not necessarily practicing a ton of self-awareness in these average levels, defaulting instead to our most familiar patterns of thinking, feeling, and behaving. Yet we're not necessarily to the point of doing overtly destructive things in the name of our ego. In these average levels, we may be judgmental, overworking ourselves, or zoning out on our phones, but we're not to the point of persecuting others, sabotaging coworkers, or brutally bullying strangers online from an anonymous account—those are patterns reserved for the unhealthy levels.

Don Richard Riso and Russ Hudson assigned each of the levels a descriptive name in their book *Personality Types: Using the Enneagram for Self-Discovery*, shown below:

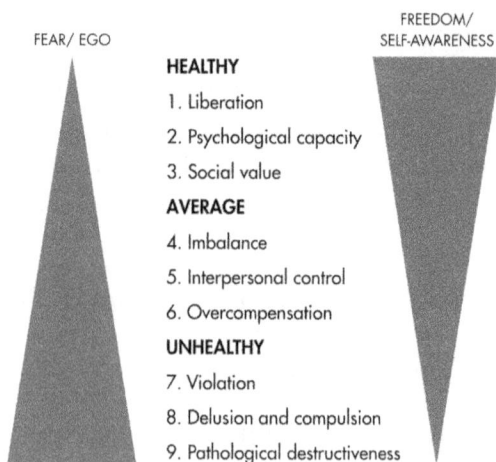

FEAR/ EGO

FREEDOM/
SELF-AWARENESS

HEALTHY

1. Liberation
2. Psychological capacity
3. Social value

AVERAGE

4. Imbalance
5. Interpersonal control
6. Overcompensation

UNHEALTHY

7. Violation
8. Delusion and compulsion
9. Pathological destructiveness

It's not crucial for you, the author, to memorize each of the nine Levels of Development for your character's type (thankfully). Instead, in the next section I'll walk you through the deterioration of each type's healthy version into its unhealthy version and what some of those steps look like along the way.

What determines where a character falls along the levels for their type is simple: their core fear's grip on them.

The core fear of each type hides in plain sight. It often doesn't look like fear. To the character experiencing it, it may look like common sense, basic caution, righteousness, or even politeness. To everyone else, it looks like distraction, intensity, obsession, and disappearing, respectively. In short, the core fear hides itself by looking like a lot of things that aren't *Ahh! That's a scary thing to me and I'm going to avoid it!*

The core fear never really goes away, but the more a person can learn to see it for what it is and live beside it, through exposure and debunking the lies it tells us, the better able they are to spend time in the healthy levels of their type.

Meanwhile, the more someone buys the lies their fear sells them and continues to call the fear by any other name, the more time they'll spend in the average and unhealthy levels. For instance, a person might tell themselves they're "just being honest" when in fact that what they're doing is being cruel to someone who triggered their insecurity (we've all see it, right?). Or they may tell themselves that not intervening when they saw someone being bullied was the best way to keep things from getting worse, when in fact they were just scared of engaging in conflict. Fear can make a compelling argument, for sure. It'll give us all the justification we need for some pretty gnarly shit.

To begin to debunk the lies their fear tells them, a character will need to risk something. We call these "stakes" in the storytelling world. What's at stake? What are the risks here?

The stakes aren't just physical danger, and oftentimes physical danger seems less risky than the *internal* stakes of one's core fear. These internal stakes look like risking rejection, risking ridicule, risking emotional vulnerability, risking being wrong, risking failure, and so on. In fact, you might find that your character would happily risk bodily harm to avoid having a difficult conversation that might make them feel abandoned. Or perhaps they'll use their body as a human shield because they're afraid that not doing so would prove they're a bad person.

Your job as the storyteller is to present your characters, especially your protagonist, with opportunities to take these risks. If they turn away, they need to face the consequences of giving their fear more space to grow and control them. If they take the risk, you need to either show them that it wasn't all that risky or that the risk was worth it. Or you make it all blow up in their face and begin their villain origin story.

This up-down movement through the levels is how a single Enneagram type can contain heroes, villains, and everything in between. The Four's healthy creativity can spiral down into a self-pitying fantasy world. The Eight's strength and desire to protect the innocent can plummet into controlling and deeply predatory behavior. The Two's generous heart can devolve into an endless hunger to be needed that causes them to rip away agency from others.

Understanding roughly where your character is in their Levels of Development can be extremely useful for you to know what to throw at them next. Are they on a growth arc or a descent into tragedy? What trigger can you throw at them to speed up the process?

Poke them with their fear and see what happens. Toss some betrayal at your Six. Make your Three fail publicly. Confine your Seven. Present unavoidable conflict to your Nine.

If they sink, they'll fall down their levels. If they swim, they'll rise up.

That's a lot of power you, the author, hold in your hands. I hope you enjoy exploiting the hell out of it.

WINGS

You can visualize the movement as side to side.

Wings are another element that can add flavor and dimension to your iconic character. Some debate exists about the best way to approach wings, so I'll present to you what I've found useful when it comes to writing them.

First, what the hell is a wing?

When we look at the Enneagram diagram, we see that the types are presented in a circle:

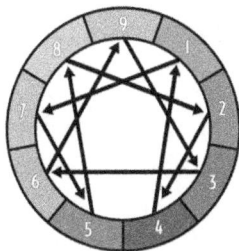

Together, they create humanity's whole perspective. Now, point to the dominant type of your character. Let's say you're writing a Five. The types on either side of that are the "wings." So, yes, Four and Six. Not too tricky. But note that because it's laid out in a circle, One is a possible wing for a Nine and Nine is a possible wing for a One.

It's common and normal for someone to take on some of the typical attributes of one or both of their wings to support their dominant type. So, a Five with a Four wing (written: 5w4) may take on some of the Four's desire to be special and strange and may show more of the outside-the-box thinking than a Five on their own. Meanwhile, a Five with a stronger Six wing (written: 5w6) is likely to be more focused on order and processes and seek more security through their cerebral approach to life.

Some people really like to chisel these wings in stone, like, "I'm a 3w4," or "this character is a 7w8." To be clear, that's fine if it helps you connect with the character, but in reality, wings aren't usually that clear cut. However, if you feel like picking a particular wing and writing to that is simpler and keeps you from getting lost in the weeds, then do that. But it's also not wrong to have a character who expresses both wings at different times or in different situations or a character that doesn't have a strong wing on either side. All of this is possible in humans, so it's possible in our characters as well.

For example, perhaps you see more of your Five's Four wing emerge when they're composing music and more of their Six wing show up when it's time to plan a heist.

It's okay not to get this deep into the details for *most* of your characters. It's even okay not to get this deep on *any* of your characters. But if it helps you write more iconic characters rather than muddying the water, then spread *your* wings and fly!

STRESS

You can visualize this movement as steam shooting through a pressure-relief valve.

When a personality is put under a lot of stress for a long time, some of its most valued and reliable patterns start to give way to the pressure. This is what we refer to as "stress" for the Enneagram.

Each Enneagram type has another type that it begins to pull patterns from after prolonged or intense stress. I like to think of this movement toward the "stress type" as a vacation from their usual ways of doing, feeling, and thinking. And as you probably know, not every vacation is restful or even fun, but it does temporarily offer us a new view.

Imagine someone is building a house frame with a hammer and nails. Eventually, it becomes time to use another tool, but this person hasn't learned about other tools yet; they might not even know they exist. When it comes time to use a drill and screws, does this person pick up the new tool or do they keep using a hammer, hitting everything harder and hoping that does the job, but causing pretty serious damage along the way?

The person who opts to try out a different tool is the person who moves toward their stress type. It's a natural way of responding to stress by at least having a new experience of it than before. I often visualize the shift as a pressure-relief valve. It doesn't solve the problems your type's patterns are creating, but it keeps the reactor from completely melting down.

Meanwhile, the person who doubles down on the hammer is someone who spirals down the levels of their type, doing real harm to themselves and others along the way. You can visualize this as the pressure-relief value not opening and the whole reactor melting down or exploding.

Each type has a particular "stress type" that it moves toward, which I'll include in the type descriptions in the next section. This is important for you to know, because your character will undoubtedly be put under stress (or should be!), and you may intuitively start writing them more like another type without even realizing it, since you've likely observed people of that particular type in your life and how they react under stress.

When you do realize that your character isn't acting quite like their usual dominant type, you might experience an *oh shit* moment. But it's very likely that you intuitively understand each type's movement toward stress, and it's flowing naturally from you.

For instance, the Eight (core fear: being harmed and controlled) will push, push, push, trying to bend the world to their will. Over time, this can wear them down, especially when they meet a situation that simply will not budge. Guess what they do in that case? Seriously, just guess. Imagine a person who's like this finally hitting that limit where they just can't keep trying to run through the same brick wall over and over again. Tap into your experience with people like this. Or, if you're an Eight, think about what you've done in the past.

If the Eight is going to spiral down the levels (keep using the same damn hammer), they might decide to simply take everyone and everything they can't control down with them in a ball of fire. ("Burn them all!" shouts the Mad King in A Song of Ice and Fire.)

But if they move toward their stress type—Five—as you may have guessed (or intuited), they'll retreat to give the situation the thoughtfulness they haven't had the space to give it yet, due to all the action they were taking. You can imagine them retreating into a cave or even a secret lair to regroup. While they're in that stress-type space, the Eight may spend the time plotting revenge, as we see frequently with many revenge plots.

Or they may be using that space to reflect productively on their previous actions. They may decide to proceed with a little less intensity next time and build in some pauses to assess whether their efforts are working. Or they might realize that it would be good to ask for outside perspectives and insights from those they trust.

What this withdrawal turns into for the Eight will depend a great deal on the tools you've given them along the way. Do they have a mentor they listen to? Do they have a trusted friend they can rely on? Have they ever hit this wall before, and if so, what did they try and how did it go?

Eventually, the character will get sick of being in that stress type, or the situation they're facing will change in such a way that they feel ready to tackle it again from the position of their dominant type. The vacation ends. It's time to take what they can from it and return to normal life.

The stress type solves a problem for each type's personality, though it doesn't always solve it *effectively*, as you can see from the example. It solves the immediate problem of "this isn't working, and I need to try something different," but the "different" can be a shitshow, too. The checked-out Nine (core fear: being cut off, separated) wakes up to all the problems they've been ignoring and is so overwhelmed that they move toward their stress type of Six and begin catastrophizing and flailing around like a Muppet. On the one hand, at least they're awake to what they've been putting off and they do have a jolt of energy that could be harnessed to effectively address the situation. But on the other hand, they may be too much of an anxious mess to think clearly, and being frantic isn't generally useful for coming up with an effective plan of attack. But, hey, at least the Nine is no longer pretending everything's fine when it's not, right? Let's call that progress.

Everyone ends up sliding toward their stress type from time to time. It's a way for us to bend without breaking. During the most intense months of the pandemic, I constantly had clients mistyping as their stress type because we were all experiencing such a new and constant state of stress. What I'm saying is that it happens to everyone, and there doesn't need to be stigma or shame around it, as it's a useful coping tool in many ways. But as a storyteller, you get to decide how best to wield conflict to develop your character and story.

Each of these movements of the Enneagram—Levels of Development, wings, and stress—are handy to know when creating iconic characters. You don't need to learn them for every type all at once, though. Notice if you're feeling overwhelmed and do less. Focus first on your protagonist, learning the ways they move through these dynamic spaces. Don't be afraid to refer back to this book as a guide until that type becomes second nature to you. Rinse and repeat.

Also, remember that not every character will have enough space on the page and in the plot to be iconic. This is good news. It means you're off the hook, but it also means that the iconic characters you do create will have the space they need to stand out. It is possible to do so much characterization of your secondary and tertiary characters that it detracts from the awesomeness of your protagonist and antagonist.

If you find yourself in the weeds with all these elements, here's my advice: forget about them. Return to the core fear and core desire of your character and write from that. It'll still provide solid, consistent characterization and give readers something recognizable to connect with.

YOU DON'T NEED TO KNOW THE ENDING IF YOU KNOW THE CHARACTERS

The amount of information a writer prefers to know about a story prior to writing it varies from person to person. That is good, that is fine, all is well with that.

Some writers kill their ability to write if they outline from start to finish first. Some can't get started until they know how it develops and ends. Some can't start until they've built an outline, even though they know they'll abandon it before the first act is over. None of these is objectively a better or worse approach. The question is simply: Where do you fall along this spectrum? How much do you need to know to be able to write the next sentence? How much is "too much" to know before you write the next sentence? Experience allows us to calibrate this for ourselves to some degree, while wisdom and self-knowledge help us avoid the trap of comparing our needs to those of other authors to see if we're "doing it right." There really is no "should" here. Whatever works for you is the "right" amount of information to proceed. (I strongly suggest you go check out Becca Syme's Better-Faster Academy offerings for speeding up the process of understanding where you fall on this spectrum and why.)

I know authors who like to write out about twenty pages of information about their protagonist before ever starting the manuscript. I also know authors who like to meet their protagonist as they draft. Regardless of where you land on the spectrum, figuring out your protagonist's Enneagram type can be a real gift to give yourself and your story.

For the heavy pre-writer, starting with the core motivations can help you develop all the backstory in an aligned way so that the character doesn't feel like a bunch of spare parts stuck together with Popsicle sticks and Elmer's Glue.

For the author who likes to meet their protagonist as they go, you can either pick an Enneagram type to start you off and see how it shows up as you write or you can start without one in mind and see which type emerges naturally as you go, and then continue to align with that type.

Either way, once you know your protagonist's type, you don't have to know how the story ends before you start (some of you will still want to, and that's okay). Your protagonist's arc will become clear. You'll start to understand that a strong ending for a One (core fear: being bad, corrupt, wrong) will likely present them with a morally gray decision to make. A strong ending for a Three (core fear: being worthless or without value) will likely present them with choosing between that accomplishment they always thought would make them feel worthy or someone who shows them unconditional acceptance regardless of their accomplishments.

The beauty of knowing a character's Enneagram type is that it becomes quite easy for you, the puppet master, to present your marionette with a potent choice at the end that forces them to show they've learned the lessons they ought to have learned through brushing up against their core fear or that they've missed those completely.

When you know your protagonist on this deep level, the ending practically writes itself.

BONUS: KEEP FROM WRITING YOURSELF OVER AND OVER

It's natural and, hell, even *fun* to write ourselves into our protagonists. We get to live a certain kind of fantasy through them that we can't live in our own skin. I'm not going to tell anyone to stop doing this. But what I will say is that unless we're committed to writing our own Enneagram type over and over again, it can be incredibly hard to create a protagonist with a distinctively different lens from ours unless we first understand what our own lens is and then internalize that other lenses are fundamentally different and just as valid.

If you don't know that you're a Four (core fear: being insignificant or without identity), or what a Four even is, you're likely to try to write protagonists who *aren't* Fours, only to saddle them with a heavy dose of your own Fourness without realizing it. It's a sort of storytelling enmeshment between author and protagonist that I see all the time and that doesn't serve the story well. It makes it tricky for us to continue writing the story sometimes, as we're trying to push it forward as if the protagonist is our type, and yet on some level we know they're not. They won't respond to the prodding we give them because the prodding is one that would motivate *us* and not *them*.

This can be a frustrating experience for an author because, without the Enneagram framework to help us decode the problem, we may know something is off but aren't able to put our finger on it.

It's incredibly difficult to view the world through the lens of another type if we don't understand 1) that we're looking through a lens ourselves, 2) that there are different possible lenses, 3) that those other lenses are just as valid as ours, and 4) what those different lenses are.

But once we open ourselves up to these new perspectives, being able to access them through our protagonists becomes much easier. Once that happens, we can write characters who are iconically not us. That's what we'll explore in the following section, where I finally hand over the goods and tell you about each of the nine types of the Enneagram. Ready to follow me down this rabbit hole? I hope you are, because once you peer through looking glass with these nine lenses, there's no going back.

SECTION 3: THE NINE TYPES

HEROES, VILLAINS, AND EVERYTHING IN BETWEEN

HOW TO USE THIS SECTION

As you read about the nine types, you'll have some questions, like, "What do I do with this information?" and "How do I pull this off?" So, before I launch into each of the types specifically, let's walk through what each subcategory you'll see means and how you can use it to your greatest advantage.

TYPE NAMES

Each of the types has a standard number, one through nine, associated with it. Those numbers are tied to the essential quality of the type (the core motivations), but the *name* associated with the type varies depending on which Enneagram ideology you're using. For instance, Type 4, which will always be tied to the core fear of being insignificant, ordinary, and lacking identity, may be called the Individualist, the Intense Creative, the (Tragic) Romantic, or many other things, depending on where you look. Don't let the names confuse you too much, though. Type 4 will always have the same core motivations, regardless of its descriptor. This is why I tend to refer to the number of the type when I talk about it instead of a particular name. The number is universal. Yes, it does require an extra step in learning to remember the difference between a Five and a Six, but because I'll be offering so many possible names for the type to you, I thought I'd stick with the one thing that doesn't change in my discussions about the types throughout this particular book.

If you're at all familiar with the Enneagram from the internet or pop culture, you're likely most familiar with the names provided by the Riso-Hudson Enneagram Type Indicator (RHETI). I used those descriptors for the types in *Reclaim Your Author Career*, and I used them along with my own writer-specific descriptors in *Sustain Your Author Career*. Or maybe you're familiar with the type names used by the Integrative Enneagram's iEQ9 Questionnaire, which anyone who signs up for my Liberated Writer 5-Week Course completes.

I honestly don't care what anyone calls any of them.

That being said, I think it's fascinating and can be incredibly useful to absorbing the nature of a type to see all the common names for each type listed out in one place. A single word, like "Perfectionist," can carry a bunch of connotations and be subject to personal experience that may lead to an incomplete picture of what the Type 1 is all about, but if I also include the descriptors of "Reformer," "Improver," and "Zealot," you'll have a better understanding of how this particular core fear can manifest in multiple ways within the same character.

So, in this subsection for each type, I'll provide a slew of words that I've seen used to describe each.

CORE MOTIVATIONS

The precise wording of core motivations can actually vary from source to source, which I find helps one grasp the understanding of the concept more than it muddies anything. For instance, Type 5's core fear is generally described as "being incompetent or incapable," which is two things, not one, right? But you start to understand that this translates into not wanting to look stupid or foolish, and then it starts to make a little more sense why one word alone wouldn't suffice.

Some cultural or personal baggage may also come along with one of the words used for the core fear or desire. For instance, Type 4 is afraid of lacking significance, and I've had more than one Four take issue with that idea. "It sounds like I need to be the center of attention all the time! That's not it at all!" But when we start to understand that significance isn't necessarily widespread attention but rather a need to feel like your existence has some meaning, the Fours usually start nodding along. "Oh, yes. That's me." Things, including people, need to mean something to the Four. They are the meaning makers as a result. That's why I define the core fear as being insignificant, ordinary, or lacking identity. The Four's fear rests in the middle of all those things, and together they give you a better sense of it.

So, in this section, I'll include not only the core fear and core desire as I believe they're best described, but I'll also provide a brief explanation that provides more context for the possible connotations of each one.

BRIEF DESCRIPTION

In this section, I'll paint a picture of how this type shows up in thoughts, feelings, and actions. I'll try to hit the meat of it, but when it comes to Enneagram, there are these things called "countertypes" within each type that have the same core motivations as the rest of the type but that manifest those motivations in notably different cognitive, emotional, and behavioral patterns.

Ultimately, I can't provide a single description that will encompass *everything* about anyone of a given type (people are too complex for that anyway), but I can hit the center of the target to provide a decent sketch, which is more than enough to set you on your way to writing an iconic character of that type.

These descriptions aren't pulled from other resources but are rather drawn from my years of reading about the types from various sources, working with the types through coaching, and writing the types in my novels.

WINGS

This subsection offers a brief description of how the wings for each type might shape the way the character appears. It's important to remember that not every character will have a strong wing, and your character may show one wing more in a particular situation and the other wing in another situation. So if we're to say someone is a 4w3 (a Four with a Three wing), that's not to say their Five wing will never make an appearance. It just means we see a lot more of the Three wing.

This section will provide some basic characteristics, but remember that the type isn't defined by the characteristics or traits but rather the core motivation.

A guiding question, when working with wings, is: "How are this wing's motivation and typical qualities being used to support the motivation of the dominant type?"

For example, in an 8w9, you might ask: "How are the Nine-ish qualities of, say, connection, conflict avoidance, calm, or common ground being used to support the core motivation of the Eight to be independent and avoid being harmed and controlled?"

The wings serve the dominant type. If you notice the dominant type serving the core motivation of the wings, then you're blending types, not writing wings.

The health of the character (see the following section on Levels of Development) will also influence how the wing shows up. Are they accessing the developed parts of their wing or the undeveloped parts? For instance, a Six wing could show up in the form of added anxiety and doubt (less healthy) or it could show up as loyalty and commitment to the betterment of a group (more healthy). I'll try to touch on both in the individual descriptions, but if you're curious about how each wing can show up, read about the Levels of Development of that type to get a better idea.

LEVELS OF DEVELOPMENT

As we've learned, each type can exhibit healthy, average, and unhealthy Levels of Development. Sometimes these are described as "low, moderate, and high integration." However you describe it, I'll talk about how the type will show up in a character depending on how much self-awareness they have in the moment (where they are in their Level of Development). As their core fear begins to grip a character, if they're not able to see how it's affecting them or they believe the lies it tells them, they will begin to act in ways that cut off connection to themselves, others, and the world around them. Essentially, the Level of Development a character is in depends on how able they are to remain connected to all parts of themselves and others despite their fear.

We move through the levels of our type on a moment-to-moment basis, but generally you'll keep your heroes in the "average" or "healthy" levels and your villains perform best in the "average" or "unhealthy" levels.

This is not to say that your hero won't falter and slip into unhealthy patterns of thinking, feeling, and doing, because it can be interesting when they do, but we don't want them to go so far as to be unable to be redeemed, and we don't want them to stay there for too long if we hope to keep them sympathetic.

Meanwhile, the villain can certainly be redeemed and experience some of the healthy levels of their type, but if they've inflicted the harm on themselves and others that usually comes along with an extended stay in the unhealthy levels, it may be too big of a feat for them to face what they've done and make amends, which is a necessary step toward returning to the healthy levels. In other words, they'll stay villainous.

This section will give a very general description of healthy, average, and unhealthy patterns for the type. If you're interested in more detailed descriptions, I can't recommend enough that you check out *The Wisdom of the Enneagram* by Don Richard Riso and Russ Hudson. Or visit their website at www.enneagraminstitute.com to find their breakdown of the nine levels for each type.

Meanwhile, this subsection can get you started with the basic flavor of each Level of Development for your character's type, and that may be plenty for you to take it from there.

VICE

Each type has a vice associated with it. This vice describes a specific pattern that emerges from this type's core fear. The vices arise logically from the core fear and are familiar patterns like deceit, envy, and gluttony. The vice of a type is usually the #1 issue at the heart of the character's problems. If you're ever unsure what to do next with your character, asking how the vice could cause them some more problems is a pretty good place to start. That's because no matter how much growth they experience, they will be in a lifelong battle against this vice. It's that integral to the type because it's interlocked with the core fear.

VIRTUE

As each type has a vice, each has a virtue. The virtue for the type can only be unlocked in moments when the core fear and core desire are not calling the shots. It takes some self-mastery for a character to embody their virtue, and often, when initially presented with their virtue, a type will feel an aversion to it because moving toward it requires them to lower their most prized defenses.

STRESS TYPE

In this subsection I'll describe what it looks like when the type shifts toward its "stress type." You'll see how the character responds to stress in a way that doesn't seem entirely aligned with their dominant type, yet very much is. When a character moves toward their stress type, they don't become that type. They don't take on the core fear, suddenly. Instead, they take on a flavor of that type by taking on some of the common patterns of thinking, feeling, and doing that we usually see from people of that type. This is where your character might find themselves when their usual ways of being aren't producing the effects they'd hoped for and they need to step aside to get a fresh angle on the situation.

GROWTH TYPE

As a type gains awareness of some of the unconscious patterns keeping them boxed in and begins to deconstruct those patterns, they access some of the healthier qualities not only of their type, but of another type that's connected to theirs along a line. This is called the growth type, and it can only be accessed by clearing out the blocks of the dominant type. Similarly to the stress type, one doesn't become the growth type but simply gains access to some of the healthy patterns of that type to add to their toolbox.

COMMON THEME PAIRINGS

This is where things really start to take off. Certain types tend to think about and interact with certain concepts much more strongly than other types do. This means that a particular Enneagram type might pair more strongly and naturally with a theme of, say, *courage* than others. Digging into which themes pair easily with each type can honestly fix most plot problems that authors run into. If your iconic character doesn't have natural chemistry with the themes explored in your book or series, it's going to be tricky to keep the internal tension up from one page to another. You can only have a meteor fall out of the sky so many times to keep the reader turning pages.

This subsection will show you which themes create strong interaction with characters of a particular type. You'll note that no character really has a monopoly on a theme, which allows for multiple types to interact strongly within a single theme—a useful thing to note when developing protagonist-antagonist dynamics. A One and a Six might both respond strongly to the concept of responsibility, but they'll have different ideas about it, and those ideas are where strong interpersonal conflict can be mined for story gold.

TRIADS/CENTERS

The Enneagram breaks down into three main triads, often called the centers: 2-3-4, 5-6-7, 8-9-1. Within these triads, you see certain qualities emerge. For instance, 2-3-4 is considered the "Feeling Center," and these types relate to the world with a lens of emotions first. But the Two, the Three, and the Four use emotions differently, which makes them distinct from one another (many Threes don't appear to be in the Feeling Center at all, but I'll go into that later). This section will explain about the triad each type falls into and how you might leverage it to create character depth.

INTERACTION STYLES

The interaction styles are sometimes called the Hornevian groups or social styles, depending on whom you ask. What it amounts to is a movement that a particular type tends toward in getting what they want.

There are three interaction styles: assertive, compliant, withdrawn.

Assertive types are associated with *moving against*. They **demand** to get what they want.

Compliant types are associated with *moving toward*. They try to **earn** what they want.

Withdrawn types are associated with *moving away*. They **withdraw** to give themselves what they want.

If you're writing a withdrawing type who's demanding they get what they want, you might want to call a timeout and reevaluate what's happening.

The energies of the interaction styles are more felt than measured. If you're struggling to know the difference, consider how you feel in the presence of someone who's an assertive type as opposed to a withdrawing or compliant type.

Each of the centers has one of each of these styles, and I'll give a brief description of how it blends with the triad of a particular type.

DIALOGUE

As wild as it may sound, the core fears and desires of each type do translate into particular ways of speaking. We can use this as a shorthand for developing characters. For example, the Five's desire to be competent and capable often translates into a speaking style of lecturing or presenting on a topic. Dialogue of this type will likely be factual and designed to subconsciously convey how smart and competent the character is. Meanwhile, the Four's desire to be uniquely themselves tends to translate into more emotion-based language that describes their subjective inner state, rather than factual knowledge. These are things that we probably recognize instinctively about people, but in the dialogue section, I'll give some tips to make sure your characters speak like themselves rather than like you.

STEREOTYPES

It's easy for us to fall into stereotypes, so this section will include what to watch out for so that your iconic character doesn't slip into a stock character. I'll also bust some myths about the type that I commonly hear.

EASY MISTAKES TO MAKE

Pretty self-explanatory. From helping authors align a lot of stories over the years, I've observed how people make mistakes for each type that lead to glitches in believable characterization, and I'll include some tips for things to watch out for as you write this type.

EXAMPLES

Because there are healthy, average, and unhealthy expressions of each type, this subsection will include heroes, villains, and everything in between. You might notice that certain types tend to be represented more as a hero, a villain, or a side character. Don't let this fool you into thinking that it's a rule. In fact, if you see that a type isn't depicted as a villain often, that might be your chance to create something that stands out, breaks the mold, and, yes, creates an even more iconic character.

Here's the caveat on this section: I'm guessing. A lot of iconic characters weren't written with the Enneagram in mind. Most of them were not. But because the author knew the type so well intuitively, they pulled off a coherent character built around a single core motivation anyway.

From the outside, we can't guess anyone's type with total certainty, nor should we when we're talking about real humans. With fictional characters, though, the stakes are much lower, and sometimes it's REALLY fucking obvious because the character will offer a literal monologue about their core fear.

So there will be iconic characters that you think about that aren't included under any of the types (maybe I don't know that character or maybe I do but couldn't decide which type they fall under). Mostly, I'll try to stick to characters who I feel about seventy percent or more confident on their type from the things they do and say. For instance, I would literally fistfight anyone who tried to tell me that Daniel Plainview from the movie *There Will Be Blood* isn't a Type 8. (And you better believe I'd be doing a Daniel Plainview impression as I yelled, "I will bury you underground!") So, there are some I would stake quite a bit on being a particular type. This doesn't mean I'm definitely right, so if you feel like it's off, that's okay. I'm open to the debate if you ever see me at an event.

For the examples in this subsection, I'll pull not only from books but from movies and TV shows as well. There tends to be more shared knowledge of movies and TV shows than books on the whole, is all. I'll do my best to keep the references somewhat popular and current while providing a diverse selection. In cases where there's a movie version of a book, say, I'll specify which version of the character I'm using for the type, as that can certainly change from one medium to another (not to mention remakes).

DEEP DIVES

For each type, I'll provide a detailed analysis into a particular iconic character of that type. The purpose is to help you see 1) how I arrived at the conclusion of the character's type, 2) how that type shows up in interesting ways, and 3) how a character of that type is important for the story's unfolding.

Deciding which characters to analyze for the following deep dives turned into a bit of a knotty problem. First and foremost, the characters I picked needed to be strong representatives of their type; they couldn't be a mishmash. It's possible that none of these characters were written with the Enneagram type in the storyteller's mind and were instead written by intuitive or observant people who simply recognized that certain clusters of thinking, feeling, and doing tend to show up together. On top of my degree of confidence that a character was a particular type before selecting them for an analysis, I was also searching for characters that have enough meat on their bones for me to sink my teeth into. That eliminated quite a few from the get-go.

It was also important to include characters with diverse backgrounds, because that can help us understand how the core fear might show up in unexpected ways in different cultural contexts. The way the world sees you and treats you certainly colors your lens on the world.

I hope that what I've come up with in these deep dives helps storytellers of *all* backgrounds gain a deeper understanding of what each type looks like within a particular character arc.

Some of these characters are heroes, some are villains, and some are antiheroes. Some have a happy ending and some make decisions that end in tragedy. Some are healthy, some are average, and some are ... iffy. The genres are all over the map, too.

You may find yourself frustrated if the deep dive I offer for a particular type is in a genre you don't like or with a character unknown to you or whose background annoys you in some way. I understand not everyone will want to sit and watch horror or read an LGBTQ+ coming-of-age book. I found this quest to be challenging in the best kind of way, and I hope you'll be inspired to push yourself as well. Delving into characters you wouldn't normally engage with for the sake of a close reading or close viewing is incredibly rewarding. It's in the places we rarely explore that we can find the most interesting gems to bring into our own stories.

Assume there will be some spoilers in each of the deep dives. Such is the nature of analyzing a story arc. In the case of characters in TV shows, I did us all a favor and kept my analysis to the first season of the show. That way, if you haven't watched it yet, you can theoretically do so without it taking up too much time (though it was tempting to analyze Dean Winchester's [8w7] fifteen-season arc in *Supernatural*, I gotta say). Also, when I spoil a big plot twist in my analysis, as in the case of my Type 6 analysis of a lesser-known (but iconic) character, I'll give you advance notice so you can watch the season and enjoy it *before* reading the deep dive.

My hope is that the deep dives will show you just *how* deep the Enneagram can take you in getting to know your characters at a core level.

ONE FINAL NOTE

It's crucial to our understanding of this framework that we remember this one thing: any description of how a particular Enneagram type manifests is a template to work from. The only true constant about a particular type is the core fear and desire.

This means that not every person of a particular type will exhibit every pattern described, and just because a character exhibits one or two patterns commonly associated with a particular type doesn't mean that that *must* be their dominant type.

For instance, if a character tests their friends' loyalty, that doesn't on its own indicate that the character *must* be a Six (fear: lacking support and guidance). Maybe they're just in a situation where knowing whom you can trust is the difference between life and death.

Similarly, if your character has a strong sense of justice, that alone doesn't indicate that they *must* be a One (fear: being bad or corrupt) or an Eight (fear: being harmed or controlled). Maybe they find themselves in a particularly unjust situation that demands their attention.

The Enneagram motivation is the basis for how we filter all of the information around us to make sense of things and keep ourselves safe, but it's not the full picture of any individual person or character, especially not on a moment-to-moment basis.

All right. Enough teasing. Let's get to it.

THE FEELING CENTER

TYPE 2

TYPE NAMES

The Helper, the Perspective of Love, the Compassionate Helper, the Altruist, the Pleaser, the Enabler, the Caretaker

CORE MOTIVATIONS

Fear: of being unworthy of love and unwanted

Desire: to be worthy of love and wanted

The Two's motivations present as helping others to earn love. Not believing anyone could want them just because of who they are, the Two seeks out situations and relationships where they are needed to avoid the possibility of rejection. The Two yearns for the relief that comes from being needed and appreciated by others.

BRIEF DESCRIPTION

Twos are keenly attuned to the needs of the world around them. They often know what a person needs before the person identifies their own need. They crave love and view it as something that must be earned, usually through care of others or their ability to help in the ways that endear others to them, and so they dedicate themselves to earning it. They tend to overlook their own deeply loving nature, labeling caring for their own basic needs as "selfish," as it takes time away from caring for the needs of others. Twos become emotionally attuned to the world around them, always on the lookout for where their help might be appreciated.

This pattern can become a need to be needed that blurs the line between help and enabling as it transforms into people pleasing in a desperate attempt to be loved by others the way they love others.

When their fear of being unworthy of love is allowed to grow unchallenged, they can draw others into codependency and "help" those who might be better off learning how to help themselves.

The Two can slip into emotional manipulation and even a martyr complex when they finally hit their wall of giving, or the giving is firmly rejected. Feeling completely depleted, they look around to find that no one is offering to help *them*. As the pattern of codependency develops, Twos whittle their circle down to exclude people who *don't* need them and include only those (often adults) who will gladly accept the assistance without turning it away. So, when the Two looks around, they often aren't entirely incorrect that no one is offering them help; relationships with those who would have done so have withered from neglect.

Twos struggle to accept help even when it's offered. As they tend to sort the world into selfish/caring and define their own thoughts, feelings, and actions as loveable/unlovable, accepting help from others may feel like points off toward their goal of earning love. As a result, they'll reject offers of help on impulse (the very thing that offends them when others do it). The unhealthy Two falls victim to pride, believing that help is something others need, not them. This pride leads to resentment, deferred dreams and ambitions, and medical issues.

When the Two challenges their need to be needed and their belief that they must earn the same basic care they offer to others freely, they begin to embody unconditional love—literally love without conditions, including the condition of being "needed" or "helpful." They are able to offer themselves unconditional love, which allows them to offer it to others as well, and for longer, as they're not exhausting themselves by always giving and never saving anything for themselves or forbidding themselves from receiving care from others. The healthy Two pours their love into themselves, others, and the world, but also requires that those in their lives share love freely where they can. The codependency gives way to interdependency, and the Two can finally enjoy their flowers for the beacon of love they are without having to earn it.

WINGS

2w1

The One wing may add structure and purpose to the Two's impulse to be needed. This type will look a little more disciplined and may also lean even harder into denying their needs, creating an elevated risk of burning out, as exertion becomes equated with being loveable and wanted. This wing may also cause the Two to be more critical of themselves and others, just as it can help them better discern who needs their help and who would be better off learning to help themselves. While Twos love appreciation, the One wing is likely to make the Two feel more ashamed of wanting it, pressuring them to help as anonymously and inconspicuously as possible as the "right" way to give.

The One will pull the Two slightly out of the Feeling Triad, balancing it with the Action Triad, meaning the Two may be able to tap into their gut instincts more easily when the need arises.

2w3

The Three wing will increases the Two's need to be recognized and seen for their efforts, which can create internal tension with the Two's belief that they must appear a humble servant to be worthy of love. They tend to have a stronger need to be influential as a way of feeling needed. 2w3s also tend to be more extroverted and charismatic, knowing how to help in a way that makes them generally likeable, so they tend to end up visible helpers in their community, leaning more heavily into the flattery common to the Two.

The Three wing keeps the Two firmly planted in the Feelings Triad, which increases the focus on worth and the craving for attention and recognition.

LEVELS OF DEVELOPMENT

Healthy: Feels unconditional love for others *and self*, empathetic, attuned to the needs of others, gives out of love and abundance rather than to earn appreciation, maintains clear boundaries and is able to accept help, flourishes in *interdependent* relationships.

Average: Gives to ingratiate or people-please, needs to be needed, sensitive to rejection of their service, forces help upon others, becomes possessive of those who have received their help, acts self-important based on ability to give more than others.

Unhealthy: Relies on forced reciprocation to manipulate others, feels entitled to appreciation after giving, refuses help from others then plays the martyr, frequently feels victimized, acts helpless or fakes illness to receive help from others without having to ask.

VICE

The vice of the Two is **Pride**. This is expressed through the Two's belief that *others* are the ones with needs and who benefit from help, and that the Two doesn't require the same care. It also shows up in the Two believing they know what's best for another person, even when the other person disagrees. The vice leads to power imbalances, codependency, and the Two running at a deficit that can't last.

Your Type 2 character will get themselves into trouble by trying to help others beyond their capacity while also rejecting help from others.

VIRTUE

The virtue of the Two is **Humility**. Only once the Two begins dealing with their vice of Pride, which tells them they don't need the same care as others and they are better at helping than others, can they begin to experience a state of Humility. This allows them to accept the care they need from themselves and others without it wounding their pride. Existing in Humility means allowing that the world can get along without them, even if it's better with them in it.

STRESS TYPE

Moves toward Eight. When the Two's efforts to help either go unappreciated or are rejected for too long, this can push the Two into taking on some of the forcefulness and need to exert control over others from the Eight. Believing they know what's best for everyone, the Two may force people to accept their help, not taking no for an answer. They may find ways to render those around them helpless so that they are needed.

Or they may go in the opposite direction and say, "Fine, if you won't let me help you, you're on your own!" and chop off their connections with others, stepping away from codependence into the Eight's "every man for himself" hyper-independent attitude. If the Two can reconnect with some of their deeper yearnings during this time of independence and tend to their own needs, they can move out of their stress type with more clarity on what they need from others, not just what others need from them. They can also return more in touch with their physical needs, which

Twos tend to repress "in service" to helping those around them.

GROWTH TYPE

As the Two stops fearing their own needs and emotions, they are able to access some of the authenticity and self-knowledge of the Four. Considering their inner state no longer feels like a threat, and they are able to accept and express more of the complicated and needful parts of their nature.

COMMON THEME PAIRINGS

Love, commitment, connection, responsibility, worthiness, generosity, pride

TRIAD/CENTER

Heart/Feeling/Emotions

Twos are strongly attuned to the emotions of those around them. Their own emotions are less reliably available to them, as tuning into those might alert them to needs of their own that aren't being met, which threatens their ability to serve others continuously.

Twos frequently attempt to help themselves (covertly) through helping others who are struggling with the same thing. This may look like offering a shoulder to cry on to the person going through a divorce instead of dealing with their repressed emotions around their own recent divorce. It could look like working with at-risk youth as a way of fully feeling the unacknowledged emotions from their own rough childhood. Twos will give you the hug they wish someone would give them as well as the advice they need to hear. Until they allow themselves to receive the hug and attune to their own emotions, though, they may end up giving the help *they* need rather than the help the *other* person needs.

Shame/Worth/Attention

Twos fall into the trap of believing love (for them, at least) is conditional and that they must perform particular acts to be worthy of receiving any. This can lead to the subconscious belief that any hour, minute, or second when they are not earning love through selfless acts, they are unworthy of love. While Twos will give as a form of soothing their own core fear and striving toward their core desire, they do also need reassurance from others that their efforts are working. They want to be *seen* as helpful as much as they want to know that they are helping. The attention that they need is less about an audience (sometimes it's about an audience) and more about the human need to be recognized. They crave having their true selves be seen deeply and approved of, though the risk of allowing others to truly see them and possibly face their disapproval is nearly impossible to stomach and causes the Two protect themselves with a façade of helpfulness and caring. Unfortunately, the Two may subtly learn that the only part of them people approve of is the helpful part, not because that's the truth, but because that's all the Two allows the world to see of them.

INTERACTION STYLE

Twos are a **compliant** type. They believe they must earn the attention and affection they want through being needed and helpful. They often believe that they must earn the right to attend to their own needs and emotions by attending to everyone else's first, and they hope that in helping others, they'll receive the same kind of care in return without needing to ask.

DIALOGUE

The Two's need to be helpful doesn't stop at speech but rather flows into the way they communicate with others. When writing dialogue for a Two, include advice, both solicited and unsolicited. The compulsion to help and their gift to spot where people need help may look like, "You should tell her how you feel," or "Go lie down, you need some rest." We've all been on the receiving end of unsolicited advice, and sometimes it's a nice gift, but often it feels like criticism or an insult, a presumption that we can't take care of ourselves.

Twos are also big on encouragement, which is generally a *helpful* way of speaking to others. It's nice to have someone encouraging you, and the Two knows this. It's something they can offer. Twos therefore frequently assume the position of cheerleader, encouraging others to strive for their dreams and offering praise and confidence that others are capable of whatever they put their mind to: "You're exactly who needs to be doing this," or "I know you got this, and I can't wait to see it!" A Two is a nice friend to have. However, this praise and encouragement can drift into people pleasing, and the Two's desire to be liked can lead to unfounded or forced compliments that cross the line into clear emotional manipulation.

This people pleasing is vocalized through flattery to those to whom the Two wishes to endear themselves and earn approval from in return. This may be a compliment for everyone in the room: "I love those shoes!" or "You're seriously a genius." Because the Two is so attuned to the emotional needs of others, they know exactly what other people need to hear and may offer that rather than what is particularly true. This may work for a while, but when the receiver of the flattery catches on to the disingenuous praise, they may stop trusting the Two's words and reject their offer of verbal help—a painful experience for a Two.

STEREOTYPES

Twos are often depicted as pushovers or softies. Their caring nature may even make us inclined to imagine a woman, but there are plenty of male Twos out there who have learned how to earn love in socially acceptable ways for their gender.

Twos are also often depicted as sweet, needless side characters who have no dreams of their own. Perhaps the Two has repressed their dreams because having individual dreams feels selfish, but Twos still dream of their own achievements. The reason this stereotype persists is that the Two often falls into a pattern of allowing themselves to pursue their own dreams *only* once everyone else is taken care of and if the Two's dreams don't seem too selfish (so, very rarely). The idea of Twos being soft is incomplete as well, as Twos can also be incredibly fierce in their love, to the point of being possessive, jealous, and unyielding. They can become scary to protect those they love, if that seems like a solid route toward earning more love.

Another stereotype of Twos is that they are a perpetual servant, but they can also go through periods of staunch independence, where they feel the need to tell everyone to go fuck themselves. This is usually a result of some sort of breaking point after they've encouraged too many people to rely on them, as the pendulum swings from codependency to hyper-independence. This period can last for a while, as the Two becomes unable to see a route toward connection that doesn't include the codependence that burned them so badly.

So, while the stereotypical Two has a whole network of people relying on them, it's also possible to meet a Two in their "fuck off" state before they start to discover the middle ground of interdependence.

EASY MISTAKES TO MAKE

Twos are rarely elevated to protagonist roles in stories and are often shunted to the side to play supporting roles. It's not hard to see why authors might naturally do this, since Twos do like to support and care for others, but authors miss a huge opportunity by only giving them that overdone part to play. Twos can drive their own story easily, especially since they tend to refuse help from others. Don't phone it in by always assuming that your Two should take a passive, supporting role where they show up whenever your protagonist needs them. They have an inner world of their own, and not every Two is up for helping every person all the time. They, too, often select who's worthy of their help and who is not.

EXAMPLES

Diana Prince/Wonder Woman (2017 film), Ted Lasso, Peeta Mellark (Hunger Games), Sookie Stackhouse (*True Blood*, TV series), Samwise Gamgee, Molly Weasley, Lysa Arryn (A Song of Ice and Fire), Annie Wilkes (*Misery*)

DEEP DIVE: TED LASSO

For this analysis, I'm focusing solely on Season 1 of the television series Ted Lasso *and the development included in it. It felt important to use a male example for Type 2, because it's so rare to see that depicted. The rarity of seeing a strong (healthy) male Type 2 is, I'd argue, an important factor in why he's such an iconic character. It's also why the show took off like it did during a time (2020) when the world felt like a particularly uncaring place led largely by uncaring men and many American viewers were isolated and starving for kindness and connection. As I'll show in the following deep dive, Twos bring nurturing and compassion that is sorely needed in the cutthroat, tough-guy version of masculinity that defines a male-dominated organization like the English Premier League. The effect is that Ted stands out even more starkly in the audience's mind against that backdrop and his Two-ness shines like a lighthouse through a foggy night.*

Analysis: For the uninitiated, Ted Lasso is a fish-out-of-water story about an American football coach who is deliberately hired to fail as a coach in the English Premier League (that's professional soccer to Americans; football to almost everyone else). When we first meet American Ted Lasso, as his flight lands at the airport where he's set to take on his new role, he seems like a bit of a naïve bumpkin with his colloquialisms and complete lack of knowledge about football (soccer). But almost immediately, we get a taste of something else from him, something richer and refreshing against the uptight and proper backdrop of English culture. As Ted leaves baggage claim, he refuses to allow the hired chauffeur, Ollie, to carry his bags. Not only that, he asks for Ollie's name and remembers it.

This tells us two important things about Ted: he doesn't like accepting help, and he sees people as people, regardless of their position in life—both essential qualities of the Two. As for the first indicator, it may be that Ted's refusal to let Ollie carry his bags is the result of the Two's knee-jerk reaction to refuse help, displaying the vice of the Two, Pride. Twos want to see themselves as needed and helpful, and accepting help from others or needing others feels like points off on their lovability rating. But it's also possible (and probably more likely) that Ted's refusal to let Ollie carry his bags is a result of his type's virtue, Humility, resulting from the ability to see that Ollie is just like him regardless of status, and Ted's choice to not off-load heavy bags to the chauffeur is a sign of respect for his equal humanity. It could also be a little of both.

Twos tend to make an effort to remember the names of those around them because they know how special it makes someone feel to be remembered. Sometimes, the impulse here is to show love to people in small but important ways, and sometimes the impulse is born out of the pattern of flattery that Twos fall into, which is an attempt to earn love and appreciation from others, thereby creating a strong bond so that the Two soothes their deep fear of rejection. Winning people over is certainly something we see Ted not only do but enjoy like a sport throughout the season. Is it flattery, or is his heart so full that he can't help but spread love to those around him? Again, it's probably a little of both.

But you'll notice that he has a knack for spotting people with their walls up and enjoys trying to break those walls down. We get a taste of this when the hard-to-impress reporter Trent Crimm stands up to speak and Ted immediately disarms him with a compliment about his glasses. We see it again when he says, with regard to aging star player Roy Kent's grumpiness, "He thinks he's mad now. Wait till we win him over."

While the niceness often brightens someone's day, it's also a defense mechanism for Twos. It protects them from their vulnerability of rejection. Flattery is a form of emotional manipulation, trying to control the interaction to avoid experiencing pain. Killing someone with kindness is still the result of homicidal intent, after all. Twos might call it self-defense, if they realize they're doing it.

Occasionally, we see Ted go so far out of his way to people-please and win people over that it's clearly less about what others want and more about reinforcing his appearance to himself and others of being a helpful and considerate person —holding the door open for Rebecca when she still has quite a ways to go to get to the exit, baking her biscuits (cookies) from scratch because he knows she likes them, and eating Indian food that's way too spicy to keep from embarrassing Ollie in front of his in-laws. Is Ted also doing the last to perform his niceness for Trent Crimm, the prickly reporter he's dining with? It's entirely possible. Yet it could just as realistically be that Ted is doing it to perform for *himself* as a way to reinforce his identity as a loving and self-sacrificing person.

The question becomes: *What* is Ted sacrificing to continue believing he's a helpful and caring person? Oftentimes, the answer is honesty.

If you were to pick a single gift that Ted Lasso possesses, however, you would probably name his ability to know what people need to hear. Not what they *want* to hear (that would be the gift of a Three), but what they *need* to hear. In this way, he's able to heal people, often against their will. He knows what the hotshot player Jamie Tartt needs to hear after being berated by his father following the last game of the season, and Ted offers that gift in the form of a supportive letter. He knows what Roy Kent needs to hear to step up into a leadership position, and he delivers that message via Madeleine L'Engle's *A Wrinkle in Time*. Ted sees the world through the lens of the needs of others, and he genuinely takes pleasure and finds self-esteem in his ability to fill their needs.

Then there's his relationship with his wife back in America, the biggest peek we get into Ted's personal life. His marriage isn't going so well. It wouldn't make sense, knowing what we do about him, for Ted's marriage to be on the rocks because he *doesn't* give her enough attention or isn't supportive or encouraging; those are common reasons for marriage problems, but nothing we'd expect from a Two. The conflict between them is, instead, that she needs *more* space. He's too giving, too nice, too soft, too malleable …

There's no bad blood, no emotional neglect or abuse, only an amicable falling out of love on her part with a man who knows nothing *but* amicableness. Ted's pattern of self-sacrifice is most pronounced in this relationship, as his Two's tendency toward codependency and clinging in a

73

romantic relationship triggers his defense mechanism of repression. Because he's fairly healthy, he recognizes that trying to pull her closer will only drive her away, and love means giving the person what they need, even if that's not what you need (this is a SUPER-healthy mentality for a Two and rare to see), and so he gives her an entire ocean's worth of space.

But make no mistake, his decision to give her space is *also* an attempt to stay connected to her any way he can. It's actually a last-ditch ploy to hold on. An argument could be made that he does it out of desperation and a fear of being *entirely* rejected when all is said and done. It's unclear if that's his motivation behind it, and it's likely he doesn't himself know his true motivation.

His marriage troubles clearly eat at him, and his response is generally to bottle up his fear and sadness, repress them, and work even harder to make the people around him feel good. The result of that is typical of Twos who try this: it leads to a psychosomatic event—a panic attack.

Ted Lasso's core fear (being unloved and unwanted) is most clear in the way he forces his help on people who don't ask for it and sometimes don't want it. Do they usually end up appreciating it? Sure. But it's sometimes said that unsolicited advice is criticism, and Ted offers plenty of unsolicited advice wrapped in a nice, folksy bow.

There are two times in the season when we see a typical pattern of the Two's core fear play out in the form of sparing someone the pain of having to reject him by sending them away first. This is an advanced maneuver of a Two that accomplishes their aim of reassuring themselves that they always put others first while also sparing them the pain of hearing the other person outright reject them. It deprives the other person of an opportunity for personal growth and honesty, but the Two isn't as concerned with that, as, again, Twos are often okay with sacrificing honesty for the sake of their image as a nice or generous person.

Ted pulls this maneuver first with his wife (who, unsurprisingly, he has a safe word with when one wants to hear the un-sugarcoated truth from the other), when he tells her that she doesn't have to keep trying to love him like she did at the start of their relationship. He does a selfless thing by letting the woman he loves go. He offers her relief and freedom at the cost of his own need for being loved. It's a great display of self-sacrifice, but is it done to spare her pain or him? Because he doesn't particularly address that well of emotion until the panic attack forces him to. Either way, this is something that most Twos wouldn't consider giving to someone else. I would argue that it's a true sign of his love for her in this case, but the way he goes about it is also an attempt to spare himself pain by being the one to "call it."

The second time he pulls his maneuver is at the end of the season when he walks into Rebecca's office and already has a letter of resignation ready to go to spare her the pain of having to fire him. Even when his marriage or career is on the line, he is always thinking of how to help those around him, rather than experiencing his own emotions about the situation. Perhaps it's out of genuine care for the other, but perhaps it's to spare himself the pain of being rejected. It's hard to tell and probably a little of both, considering where Ted tends to fall along the Levels of Development for his type.

Ted starts the season at a fairly high level of health due to his self-awareness. We see very healthy moments of the Two shine through in almost every episode, so he certainly has those within his bandwidth. His ability to see past people's walls and into their pain allows him to avoid taking most rejection too personally, and he certainly faces a lot of it when he first arrives at Richmond FC. His connection to a down-to-earth humility keeps his ego from becoming a problem most of the time. We certainly see moments of him slip into average levels of health, like when he devotes his attention to winning over people who don't like him, which steals attention away from deepening connection with the people who already do (this is typical of a Two, especially a 2w3 like Ted).

I can't stress enough how unusual it is to see a protagonist who is this healthy for their type. The problem writers run into is that there isn't much room for growth when the protagonist is already so healthy. I would argue that it works for this show because the *appeal* of the show is so clearly how we can show up for each other and how love and hope can heal us. Ted is the gravitational center that the other characters orbit. Not only is Ted's narrative job to give the love and care that the team needs to become the best versions of themselves, but it's to also inspire the viewer to try to do that as well.

Ted Lasso is a show of EQ, one that models healthy behavior in a way that is rare to see in a comedy and on television at all, especially in a time when the news is full of cruelty, fear, and low EQ.

Ted still has small lessons to learn, which allows others to step up for him like he steps up for them and to reciprocate his care, the effect of which is that the audience is left chock-full of serotonin and oxytocin. But he is almost never a low-average Two, let alone an unhealthy Two. This keeps him sympathetic but also someone we look up to.

In general, I warn authors away from starting the story with your protagonist being too healthy, because it does limit how much they can grow, but if you want to ignore that advice, Ted Lasso is a useful template to follow for starting off with a healthy protagonist who allows room for less healthy secondary characters to learn, change, and grow right before our eyes. This makes for a feel-good story all around and helps us see others through Ted's eyes, so that every wall we encounter becomes an invitation to reach out and see what pain lies locked away and how we could become our better selves to support others in healing their wounds.

Ted Lasso is an iconic character who showed up at the right time in culture to take a show that might have disappeared beneath the avalanche of content we're drowning in were it to have been released a few years earlier or later than it was. As it is with comedy, so it is with writing iconic characters: timing is everything, and the writers of *Ted Lasso* got it right on both counts.

TYPE 3

TYPE NAMES

The Achiever, the Competitive Achiever, the Productive Perspective, the Motivator, the Role Model, the Performer, the Status Seeker

CORE MOTIVATIONS

Fear: of being worthless, of lacking value

Desire: to have worth, to be valuable

The Three's motivation presents visibly through doing, creating, and achieving what others (usually those with the Three's desired status) will find valuable, praise, and admire.

BRIEF DESCRIPTION

Threes are driven by a need to achieve. They want to be the best at their chosen game. What the game is will vary, but they are always playing one. They may consider others their opponents, but the game may also be a solo one, where they are playing against themselves. Maybe the game is to hit a goal, to accomplish something that others find impressive, or to achieve something that hasn't been done before. Maybe the game is beating others for a promotion or earning the highest commissions.

For Threes, the rules of the game are usually set by other people, then the Three enjoys finding the most effective way to play, exploiting loopholes and stress-testing those rules to see if they can be bent to achieve the ultimate goal. Threes want to impress others and earn praise for their savvy and efforts. As a result, they develop an ability to know who others want them to be and to don that persona as needed. They are keenly aware of how others see them, which helps them perform the role that is most likely to be valued in a particular setting.

Problems arise for the Three when they get so adept at performing for others that they lose touch with who they are behind the curtain. Over time, the praise they receive for playing their role reinforces their fear that if they showed their full, authentic self, it would be rejected and ruin what status they've secured for themselves. As a result, Threes lose touch with who they are outside of the roles they play, like boss, soldier, father, daughter, and so on.

Threes tend to view the world in terms of success and failure. Was that project a success? If they take that risk, will they fail? They will pull out all the stops to avoid the feeling of failure, because for the Three, it's often not "that project failed to meet the target," but rather "I'm a failure because that project didn't meet the target." The emotional stakes of success can blind the Three to all else.

Because the Three is so hungry for praise and admiration, they can struggle to properly credit others for their success, preferring to stand alone as a self-made person. When this happens, they're usually on the way to a downfall, as others, feeling underappreciated, may withdraw the support that helped the Three thrive. If the Three can lessen their tunnel vision around gaining external recognition, they can begin to have a clearer picture of what they value, rather than what society values, and strive for that in a healthy and meaningful way. Only once the Three begins to ground themselves in their own long-forgotten desires rather than always viewing themselves through the desires of those around them can they begin to explore who lives behind the masks they wear and start to value those parts of themselves that they've kept hidden, allowing the Three to bring an authentic self forward that inspires others and is truly worthy of awe and appreciation.

WINGS

3w2

The Three with a Two wing often seeks influence and worth through serving as a mentor for their community. They are likely to pluck people from the crowd to elevate to their level of success, which certainly helps others, but also serves the psychological need of reinforcing their higher status and success in comparison to the group. The Two wing gives the Three a warmth that pulls them more into the interpersonal sphere and can keep them from making decisions that benefit themselves but harm others in their pursuit of a goal.

The Two wing keeps the Three focused on the emotions of others, but doesn't necessarily help them pause to tap into their own feelings, which the Three tends to leave behind in their race toward success and achievement.

3w4

The Four wing can be an anchor for the Three in that it reminds them to check in with what they want, not just what other people want them to want. This is a leg up in helping them connect to their authentic self, once the public performance of success wears them out. The Four can also add a desire for the Three to not just be successful and accomplished, but be successful and accomplished in a special way that sets them apart from all the other successful and accomplished people in the world.

The Four wing adds an emotional sensitivity to the Three that redirects some of their attention toward their inner world, which can help them share their story in an inspirational way, even as it can encourage them to talk all about their lives in a self-promotional way.

LEVELS OF DEVELOPMENT

Healthy: In touch with their heart and authentic, inner-directed, self-assured and benevolent, motivating and inspirational, highly effective and efficient.

Average: Overly concerned with performance, bases self-worth on accomplishments, competitive and compares oneself with others, salesy and disingenuous, image-conscious social chameleon, braggadocious and attention seeking.

Unhealthy: Exploitative and opportunistic, cutthroat desire to feel superior, vindictive with a desire to destroy others for a more favorable comparison, strongly narcissistic, sometimes exhibits psychopathic behavior.

VICE

The Three's vice is **Deceit**. This shows up as presenting a highly curated image of themselves to the world that omits and obscures anything considered unflattering or unimpressive. Who they present themselves to be becomes dependent on what's rewarded in the environment. The vice also shows up in the form of self-deceit, where the Three can no longer access their authentic self and becomes afraid that there is nothing below the image they present to the world.

Your Type 3 character will get themselves into trouble by performing a false version of themselves that they cannot maintain over the long run and that others may catch on to as false.

VIRTUE

The virtue of the Three is **Veracity**. Only once the Three can own up to how they're deceiving themselves and others through projecting a curated image to the world can they begin to experience a state of Veracity or authentic truthfulness. This allows them to stop performing, understanding that their innate value speaks for itself and that even their "unimpressive" parts have inherent value and are worth embracing.

STRESS TYPE

Moves toward Nine. When the Three gets caught up in measuring their worth by their productivity, they begin to exploit themselves as one might a worker robot, leaving human emotion completely out of the picture. The praise and approval they do receive from others doesn't land the way they'd hoped, since the Three is emotionally and spiritually detached from their work. This moves them toward the tuning out and lethargy of the Nine. It's not uncommon for stressed Threes to spend long hours on the couch, bingeing TV or video games, as their self-worth, which has become attached to productivity, bottoms out. If they can use this time to rest and this distance from action to reconnect with what their feelings are trying to tell them, they can transition away from stress toward a healthier pace of productivity that is anchored in authentic expression and therefore beneficial rather than degrading to their sense of self-worth.

GROWTH TYPE

As they release their consuming need for personal recognition, the Three is able to focus more on the success and security of others through accessing their growth type, the Six. They move from *me* to *us*, understanding that they didn't get to where they are alone, and that they have a stronger sense of self-worth when they work in service to others.

COMMON THEME PAIRINGS

Success, achievement, worth, value, exploitation, individualism, image, authenticity, connection, status

TRIAD/CENTER

Heart/Feeling/Emotions

While the Three is in the emotion triad, it's rare to find a Three who looks or feels like a heart-based person. The way the Three relates to their feelings is that they generally don't. It's not that Threes aren't deeply feeling people—they most definitely are, and their desire to achieve is an offshoot of that—it's that the Three sees emotions as incredibly inefficient. Emotions work on their own schedule. When given oxygen, they can throw a wrench in one's tight timeline for achieving goals. It's hard to perform the way others want you to when you're experiencing emotions that run counter to the desires of others. So, the Three learns to set those feelings aside until the goal is achieved.

But once the goal is achieved, does the Three actually pause to feel their feelings? Nope. Instead, they move the goalposts, and those pesky emotions are never given space to come forth and deliver the important information they offer. The Three often looks like an Action Center type because of their preference to do rather than feel. Feeling involves slowing down, something that terrifies most Threes too much to even consider.

Threes often fear that if they slow down, their ambition will completely disappear, never to return. This is usually a result of their only experience with slowing down being an involuntary one where they are completely spent, burned out, and forced to confront all the unpleasant feelings they've locked away for so long. Once a Three can learn to voluntarily slow down and value emotions as the crucial information they are, only then can they start to connect with the inherent value of those parts of them they've been hiding from themselves and others.

Shame/Worth/Attention

The shame that Threes experience tends to revolve around the concept of failure. Rarely do they think of a particular project or undertaking as a failure, but rather they internalize it as "I am a failure." Their worth becomes wrapped up in being what other people think is worthy, and they end up trying to impress too many people with different, often conflicting, desires. Eventually, others catch on to the shapeshifting, and the Three might get a reputation as a chameleon or a dishonest person simply because they are trying to do what people want them to do, and different people want different things.

The Three doesn't trust that people will notice their efforts and achievements and offer the attention the Three is seeking (and they might be right), so they have a tendency to *tell* others about said efforts and achievements. In this way, they tend to be the most successful of this triad at getting the attention they're seeking. Unfortunately, what they get is literally *just* attention, not what their heart is truly after, which is being deeply seen and accepted. While being actively disliked does hurt Threes deeply, many will settle for it in a pinch if other forms of attention aren't available.

Once Threes can stop thinking of everything in terms of success/failure, they are able to shake off the shame that *they* are a failure if their efforts aren't properly recognized. They can begin to take the brave step of focusing on what they value and only settling for attention as a natural consequence of their expression of inherent worth and value, rather than a goal unto itself.

INTERACTION STYLE

Threes are an **assertive** type. They don't wait around for the attention they want; they go out and demand it. They tell people why they're accomplished, impressive, and worthy of praise so that no one will miss it. They don't believe that others will notice and admire them if they don't make themselves unmissable.

DIALOGUE

The Three's need to be recognized for their achievements can color their speech with a solid dose of self-promotion. They attempt to curate their image by keeping the conversation focused on the parts that they believe will be valued. Because Threes like to be seen as motivational, you usually won't hear about a Three's failures unless they're presented as an essential building block of a larger success story. It's very common to hear Threes say something to the effect of, "If I did it, so can you."

(Once the Three's speech includes the full story and more of their true emotional experience, it becomes authentically inspiring and motivational to others, which is one of the gifts the Three offers to the world.)

The Three's desire to meet their goals leads them to developing a talent for persuasive speech. Because they are so tapped into the desires of others, they are able to present offerings and incentives others are eager to take. Threes tend to know how to speak the audience's language. (An exception is made here from time to time when the Three's self-awareness is so low that they can't imagine anyone not wanting the status and praise they're seeking for themselves.) Threes sense what others want, and their speech often reflects that, presenting only the information that will move others in the direction the Three needs, and keeping the less appealing details out of sight. As a result, they often speak in "inspiring" mottos that display their drive for success, like, "I'll sleep when I'm dead," or "Always be closing."

STEREOTYPES

Threes are often depicted as charismatic smooth talkers, and while that can certainly be the case, they can still be empathetic people who don't *mean* to deceive others and genuinely believe that they are being valuable by offering people what they want.

Most Threes aren't actually aware of the ways they deceive themselves and others and don't necessarily consider their approval-seeking shapeshifting to be a form of deception. They tend to view it more as a matter of curating parts of themselves so that only the sliver that the other person would approve of is put on stage, keeping the rest backstage. It's hard to blame a Three for taking this approach when the rewards for it are so great and immediate.

While Threes may learn to appear confident, if that's a valued quality within their social group, they often feel exhausted about trying to keep it up. Unless they are especially talented at self-deceit, they usually understand that they are not as confident as they appear and are taking a "fake it till you make it" approach to life. Internally, the Three may feel like they're at a never-ending job interview or audition, and that can lead to deep loneliness and despair because they believe they will never be able to show themselves fully and be deeply seen and valued.

Another stereotype is that Threes have it all together and their emotions aren't a factor in their daily lives, but that's rarely the case. Threes often feel overwhelmed but react to the feeling by taking on more projects (increasing action) rather than pausing to allow their feelings to guide them toward a long-term solution. Beneath the shiny exterior of the Three is a deep well of emotion, waiting for its moment to burst forth. When the Three is mindful of that and learns to value the full range of their emotions, they become absolute magicians and achieve things that hold a deeper significance for themselves and the world around them. They can be truly inspirational. That is, if they can recognize in themselves the difference between performing feelings and feeling them.

EASY MISTAKES TO MAKE

It's easy to write a surface-level Three by reducing a character to raw ambition, but that makes for a forgettable Three. *Why* does the Three feel the need to achieve? What authentic parts of them are being left off the page? How might they surprise other characters with their sensitive heart?

As you write them, don't forget about the pain Threes carry that they are not enough if they aren't producing something that others find valuable. Don't forget that the Three may begin to exploit themselves as heartlessly a robber baron exploits the working class in their desperate and sympathetic pursuit to make something of themselves. Threes will win capitalist games nine out of ten times as a result of their default patterns, but don't be fooled into believing that it will actually scratch the itch the Three has around their value and worth. Being the best might soothe the fear-itch temporarily, but it'll only itch more after. They are *not* truly satisfied by playing the game, so don't let them be.

EXAMPLES

Dorian Gray, Don Draper (*Mad Men*), Apollo (Greek mythology), Tiana Rogers (*The Princess and the Frog*, 2009), Elle Woods (*Legally Blonde*, 2001), Aladdin (Disney's *Aladdin*, 1992), Tahani Al-Jamil (*The Good Place*), Gilderoy Lockhart, Patrick Bateman (*American Psycho*)

DEEP DIVE: ELLE WOODS

I had a hell of a time deciding on a Three to dive into, as there aren't that many aspirational portrayals of them in media, and I'm sure any Threes reading this are tired of hearing about their bad behavior. When my trawling the internet for inspiration brought me to Elle Woods, the protagonist of the 2001 film Legally Blonde, *it was a real forehead slapper moment. Of course she's a Three, and of course she's iconic.*

As I went in for a re-watch, I also found that she's refreshingly healthy and exemplifies what's so great about this type … but she's also not without faults. I was worried that a bubblegum white-feminist comedy released two months before 9/11 wouldn't hold up twenty-four years later, but outside of a few instances of words-we-don't-use-anymore, it's still got it. And more importantly, Elle is an example of a Three we can draw from who leans into her natural talents and is undeniably likeable.

Analysis: When we first meet Elle Woods, she's prepping for an expected proposal from her college boyfriend, Warner. He's the "perfect guy" by all West Coast standards of American whiteness and wealth, just as she's crafted herself to be the blonde bombshell every boy wants and every girl wants to be (heteronormatively speaking, which is how most of this story goes, since it's poking fun at traditional gender roles even while it can't quite escape them in this 2001 world). But what was supposed to be a proposal turns into Elle being dumped at a nice restaurant because she's not a "serious" enough person to be the wife of an aspiring East Coast elite politician like Warner.

This is the inciting incident of the movie, and why it works so effectively is simple: Elle thought she'd done everything to craft a "perfect" image of herself—she thought she'd played the game exactly how it was intended to be played—only to find out it didn't win her the status and approval she was seeking. This is an excellent knock upside the head to a Three, whose attention naturally flows toward performing. This could be performing a role, performing bliss, performing perfection, performing *anything* that will win approval from the intended audience of the performance. But rather than earning her praise, the superficial identities she's stacked together are now being held against her, and the thing she's after—Warner—is being taken away from her.

Elle's core fear of lacking value and worth is the engine of the film, as she begins the story building her value and worth on something she can't control, which is the approval of others. There's always someone who will be disapproving and dismiss your value, therefore the pursuit of *external* approval as a way of cobbling together a sense of self-worth is a never-ending pursuit doomed to fail. As it does for her, when Warner dumps her.

But is it *really* Warner she wants or the approval from a man like him that she wants? As the movie goes on, it becomes clearer that it was the latter. In the moment of the breakup, though, she's not thinking deeply about what she wants. She's never thought deeply about that, opting instead to do what Threes like to do, which is view themselves through other people's eyes, becoming what others want them to be, and wanting what others want them to want. In this way, Elle is lost to her authentic self, but she doesn't know it yet.

When Threes don't get what they want, they turn to competency as a means to remedy the situation. For Elle, this looks like throwing her full effort and resources into getting into Harvard Law, where Warner is headed, to show him she's a "serious" person and to win him back. Despite her curated appearance as a "dumb blonde," she pulls this off. You can't help but like her for her competency in knowing how to play the Harvard admissions system. The scene where a bunch of white men sit around a table, reviewing her video essay in which she wears a small bikini in a hot tub, and each finds a way to justify admitting her, is not only hilarious but also a great representation of the Three's willingness to understand how things *really* work in the world (not how they *should* work or how the Three *wants* them to work), and then making those things work for them. Basically, she's savvy as hell.

The next problem Elle faces is East Coast culture, represented in the movie by drab clothing, an outspoken lesbian, and a lot fewer blondes. Elle doesn't yet know how to play this game, which is evident when she shows up on Harvard's campus in eye-catching pink. Like any astute Three, she quickly notices this, and on her first day of class, we see her ditch the pink and opt for darker colors, though her jacket's still shiny (she was a fashion merchandizing major, after all). The shininess is important here, because it shows a certain degree of health. She's not rejecting *everything* that she likes to fit in (implying a strong Four wing). She still values her love of pretty things. But she's bending to fit in for the sake of achieving her ultimate goal: showing Warner she's a serious person who his family would approve of, thereby earning the proposal that was denied to her.

We see Elle slip into slightly lower levels of health once she realizes that Warner got engaged to a joyless brunette over the summer. Vivian, his fiancée, appears to be everything Elle isn't. This triggers a competitiveness typical of the low-average Three. She's ready to do whatever it takes to win. What she doesn't resort to, though, which is important for keeping her sympathetic, is tearing Vivian down or sabotaging her in any way. Instead, Elle resorts to driving herself harder to be smarter, and through that process, she starts to recognize value in herself for something *other* than 1) her appearance, 2) the roles she plays, and 3) the approval she receives from others. We start to see her use her status to help others and motivate them to go after what they want (this gifts us with the iconic "bend and snap" scene).

This story is about Elle's search for her worth in a world that offers her the cheap alternative of following the rules of what a "valuable" woman looks like. Except we all know by now that those rules are written so that every woman falls short and wastes her life trying to contort herself into the prescribed mold rather than liberating herself from it altogether. Playing the game is the surest way to lose, as Elle realizes when she's confronted with the reality that what's valuable on the West Coast isn't valued on the East Coast.

At first, she goes about addressing this fear the wrong way. She gets into Harvard by playing the game of the male gaze, which she's good at but could never fulfill her ... and ultimately fails women the older they get and the less they look like teenagers. This game is proven instantly ineffective when she meets her first professor, who's an older blonde herself and not impressed by Elle's feminine wiles. When Elle admits she hasn't done the reading and this professor kicks her out of class, it's a wake-up call for her. She can't keep performing excellence—she has to actually *be* it.

If Elle wanted to, she could let her fear take the wheel at this point in the story, which might look like dropping the class with the female professor and only taking classes from male professors she could manipulate with her sex appeal. But she chooses to face the Three's vulnerability of failure rather than run from it. She doesn't blame the professor but rather takes accountability and becomes more serious about her studies. This is where we see the shift really begin to happen, as she addresses her fear of lacking value in a productive way rather than simply trying to make herself *appear* to be the ideal East Coast, Harvard Law woman.

It is a coincidence that the character who first blocks Elle's usual approach is a blonde herself? I doubt that. This professor makes the perfect mentor and even comes back in Elle's dark night of the soul to offer the push she needs to get back in the fight by delivering the line, "If you're going to let one stupid prick ruin your life, you're not the girl I thought you were." This line jolts Elle back into a place where she remembers her value isn't based on what men think of her, pushing her out of the dark night of the soul and launching her toward the climax of the film.

As her self-esteem becomes based on something other than cultural approval, she takes her eyes off her goal of winning Warner back without even realizing it. Instead, she focuses on the murder trial she's been selected to help out with (on the side of the defense). In doing so, she discovers how service to others reminds her of her *innate* value much more than being engaged to some guy who only got into Harvard because his father pulled some strings would.

It's wonderful to see a Three in this process of self-actualization. For Elle, it looks like befriending Vivian, gaining and *keeping* the confidence of the client she's defending in the trial (even when she could have chosen to earn approval and praise from one of her professors for sharing what the client told her with the rest of the defense counsel), and speaking up for herself when her professor makes a pass at her, rather than using his sexual interest to status-seek.

Being valued for "blonde hair, big boobs" doesn't hit like it used to for Elle, now that she's learning to value her innate qualities. But she doesn't *completely* reject everything about her old self. As in any feel-good story, we see the quality that she was dismissed for having become her greatest strength when her knowledge of both fashion and gender norms helps her uncover the fact that the pool boy claiming to have had an affair with the defendant was, in fact, gay, and therefore had to be lying about sleeping with a woman.

When Elle takes over as the lead attorney for the defendant (we love an unrealistic plot point in a comedy, don't we?), we see her enter the courtroom clad head to toe in pink. No more hiding. She's a West Coast blonde who loves pink AND an accomplished and intelligent woman who cares about her client. This moment represents a reclaiming of who she is, rather than kowtowing to the audience's (those in the courtroom) expectations for her. Elle really does love pink.

On her first day of law school, Elle was presented with the quote "The law is reason free from passion." But in her speech at the end of the movie, she recognizes the role of passion—one of the gifts a Three brings when they combine self-acceptance and service with their intense, goal-focused drive—by returning to the quote. For her, the law is reason *fueled* by passion.

Confronting her core fear doesn't make Elle any less ambitious or successful; in fact, it's the thing that gives her true success and sustainable ambition. When she stops seeking approval, she discovers her authentic and innate value and the service she provides to the world by stepping into that. Elle discovers what many Three protagonists are offered over their character arc: that their authentic qualities that set them *apart* from others are not parts to run from but are instead the greatest gifts they have to offer the world.

TYPE 4

TYPE NAMES

The Individualist, the Intense Creative, the Romantic, the Artist, the Aesthete, the Tragic Victim

CORE MOTIVATIONS

Fear: of being ordinary, lacking significance

Desire: to be unique and significant

The Four's core motivations present as seeking meaning to their lives. They ask the deeper questions and want to know how they are an integral and irreplaceable part of the world around them.

BRIEF DESCRIPTION

Fours mine meaning from the world and themselves. They don't want to know why things are the way they are in a scientific cause-effect way so much as they want to discover a deeper understanding of the nature of things. This can cause Fours to retreat into their imagination and live in fantasies that spin together stories to understand what everything means. Fours like to find the extraordinary in the mundane and the mundane in the extraordinary, as well as finding beauty in ugliness and what's ugly in the beautiful.

While Fours can adjust to the superficial everyday world around them, they'll always have a distaste for it, preferring to seek out the profound, the strange, and unique. They'll also struggle to feel a *part* of the world around them, rejecting their own superficial tendencies to instead become the misunderstood outsider looking in.

Fours long to be seen deeply and understood, but their fear of abandonment and rejection causes them to construct all kinds of complications and defenses that ensure they never feel fully understood. They (unconsciously) know that if they're misunderstood, rejection and/or abandonment doesn't feel so personal. The Four's essential nature can't be rejected if the other person never truly comprehended them to begin with. At the same time, Fours do tend to personalize the behaviors of others that might not be personal at all, reading abandonment into situations where others would never find it.

The Four lives in their emotions and can slip into attaching their understanding of the world to their moods if they're not careful. When they're feeling dejected, the world is a cruel place. When they're feeling validated, the world may be full of beauty. These big swings in outlook can make relationships with others fraught, as the Four tends toward a push-pull dynamic. Push you away to preempt possible abandonment; pull you close to feel special again.

Fours long for what is true and authentic. This search inspires them to try to pin down what is true and authentic about themselves, and it can provoke an endless search if they aren't careful. Fours also often believe that the dark and melancholy is truer than the bright and optimistic, and can label things like optimism, hope, and simplicity as "superficial" or "phony." This causes Fours to overlook positivity and optimism as they seek meaning in the world and may not be able to see these qualities in themselves.

When the Four learns to observe their emotions rather than to fiercely identify with them, they can allow emotions to inform their actions rather than completely drive them, and the sense of undefined longing that the Four often feels starts to give way to appreciation and gratitude for the mysteries of life.

WINGS

4w3

The Three wing's drive for efficiency can help balance the Four's tendency to make things overcomplicated. This wing makes it more likely that the Four will implement their ideas rather than letting them exist solely in an untouchable but ideal fantasy. The Three's drive to go out and grab the attention they want can create an inner tension with the Four's belief that if they are really worthy of attention, it will find them. This push and pull can cause the 4w3 to be fickle in relationships, showing up visibly, then disappearing to see if they're pursued. The Four tends not to trust that attention is authentic if they are the one to seek it, but the Three wing amplifies their need for recognition to where waiting around for it can seem an unbearable and lonely torture.

The Three wing keeps the Four planted in the Feelings Center, but does so in a way that calls them into action as a reaction to their emotions. Sometimes this is a healthy step, and sometimes it's an avoidance tactic. Either way, these Fours tend to be more extroverted as they interact with the outside world.

4w5

The Five wing draws an already withdrawn Four even deeper inside themselves. These types tend to be more introverted, and when an emotion becomes too unpleasant, they'll kick it up into their head to think about it rather than feeling it. This can create a strong rumination cycle without resolution of the emotion. Fours tend to take what others do personally, but the Five wing adds a layer of objectivity that can allow the Four to remove themselves from the situation and analyze it more objectively.

The Five wing, situated in the Thinking Center, makes this Four appear very "thoughtful" to others. They're reserved in acting on their feelings, which can allow them more space to understand themselves and see the world as it is, not only as their moods color it to be. They use the observational power of the Five to understand what's "missing" and "broken" about themselves.

LEVELS OF DEVELOPMENT

Healthy: A self-regenerating creative, profoundly inspired, introspective, sensitive, comfortable feeling the full spectrum of human emotions, individualistic and effortlessly unique, intuitive, highly attuned to the feelings of others (not just their own).

Average: Strong sense for aesthetics, lingering melancholia, creates a heightened reality through fantasy, prone to moodiness, withdrawn, feels they are exempt from social norms, envy of others leads to justification of self-indulgence, creates fantasized versions of friends, family, and lovers (positive or negative).

Unhealthy: Withdrawn and angry at self and others when dreams and fantasies don't pan out, loses self in paralyzing shame, self-hatred arises, destroys relationships with blame and accusations, engages in self-destructive behavior, indulges in mind-altering substances as a way to escape reality, self-harm likely at the lowest level.

VICE

The Four's vice is Envy. The results from their need to be special and to stand out, which compels them to compare themselves with others. When they look at those around them, they tend to see a fantasy version of their lives, where everyone has something important that the Four is lacking. This vice also shows up through an inferiority/superiority complex, with the Four scrambling to find a comparison that's favorable to them (usually through calling someone else fake, uninspired, or inauthentic). That can only last so long, though, before the inferiority underlining it rears up again and the Four is left with little but a vague sense of longing for something everyone else seems to have that they themselves lack.

Your Type 4 character will get themselves into trouble by competing with fantasy versions of others that they can never measure up to. They may even sabotage others whom they perceive to be the cause of their inner pain.

VIRTUE

The virtue of the Four is **Equanimity**. Only once the Four can begin observing their emotions without identifying with them can they experience a state of Equanimity. As they stop allowing their Envy to dictate how they feel from moment to moment and learn to observe their moods rather than being led by them, the Four stops clinging to emotions for a sense of identity and instead finds solid ground to stand on as they use their emotions to better connect to the world, rather than isolating from it.

STRESS TYPE

Moves toward Two. When the Four's emotional distancing and aloofness don't earn them the attention and recognition they need, they can swing in the other direction, taking on the Two's tendency toward clinging and codependency. Their hunger for love and attention can become stronger than any person could possibly satisfy, which only causes the Four to try to hold on more tightly. If the Four can take this moment of closeness between themselves and others as an opportunity to spend more time considering the emotions and needs of others, they can let go of emotionally manipulating others into fulfilling their needs and instead learn to fill the needs of others in a healthier and more proactive way. This allows the Four to spend less time attending to their own hurts, which don't need as much attending as the Four gives them, and anchors them in alignment with their principles and values.

GROWTH TYPE

As the Four stops choosing fantasy over reality and lets go of their need for complication, they access more of the acceptance, structure, and pragmatism of their growth type of One. They recognize that strong feelings don't impact the world, but meaningful action does, and they're able to observe their emotions rather than being tossed around by them.

COMMON THEME PAIRINGS

Significance, meaning, beauty, identity, envy, loneliness, dependence, authenticity, purpose, obsession, dreams

TRIAD/CENTER

Heart/Feeling/Emotions

Fours' attention naturally flows inward, attuning them to their emotional state. As a result, they spend a lot of time trying to describe and express that emotional state to the world in hopes of being seen and understood. This can lead to accusations of navel gazing being hurled at the Four, which doesn't land well. The Four knows that their emotions are important information, which is true, though sometimes the Four will prioritize their feelings over another person's well-being or safety, leading to a fracture in the relationship.

Fours are sensitive people, and that sensitivity doesn't always work out well for them in a harsh world, which can lead the Four to believe there's something broken or missing in them that other people have. The result of this emotional pattern is envy, which looks like comparing themselves to others, either looking for validation that the Four is broken or missing something (inferiority) or that the Four has something others don't have that isn't being properly appreciated (superiority). Sometimes the Four can experience both of these things in the same minute, which exacerbates the big emotional swings and leaves them feeling like they're always on unsteady ground.

Once the Four stops overidentifying with their emotions and learns to observe them, the equanimity they develop interrupts the constant comparisons to others and offers deeper connection without the envy, self-hatred, or contempt that accompanied their comparisonitis.

Shame/Worth/Attention

The feeling like something is missing or broken in them causes Fours to wage a constant battle against shame. Their need to be seen and appreciated as the emotionally sensitive individuals they are can become so strong that they fear their need is *too* great and the possibility of being seen and deemed lacking feels too horrible to risk. When this happens, the Four withdraws into their own fantasy world, using it as armor to protect them from the harshness of reality. They can project this fantasy onto relationships, creating a barrier to the true and authentic connection the Four yearns for, which leaves them in a perpetual state of longing.

Their natural move to withdraw into themselves pulls them away from the possibility of being seen even as it protects them from rejection and abandonment. Instead of showing all the parts of themselves—especially the parts deemed unoriginal or simple—the Four will build their worth and sense of self upon various identities that separate them from the status quo—fandoms, political groups, kinks, obscure areas of study, or any other identity marker that they find interesting or unique.

Once the Four begins to observe and confront the shame they've internalized and can recognize how undeserving they are of it, they will be able to remain more balanced in their heart, mind, and body and will understand that they can't possibly be missing something others have because they are inextricably connected with everything and everyone.

INTERACTION STYLE

Fours are a **withdrawn** type. They withdraw inward to their imagination and moods to offer themselves the attention they crave. They don't trust the authenticity of the attention they receive when they have to ask for it, so they remain withdrawn while longing for someone important that will pluck them out of obscurity and see their unique and authentic self.

DIALOGUE

Because the Four feels like there's something missing in them, they spend a great deal of time experiencing a sense of loss. This could look like nostalgia, melancholy, or a general sense that something that *ought* to be in the present isn't (without necessarily knowing what that might be). This surfaces in their speech as lamenting. They often focus on what is off and what isn't as good now as it used to be. Fours are oriented toward the past, and this shows in their inability to stop dissecting what went wrong in a relationship or how things haven't turned out the way the Four had hoped for in life. (Not all Fours talk about this all the time, especially if they've learned to wear a cheery mask, but it's certainly a common speech pattern.) "If only..." is a common phrase to hear from them, as well as, "I just feel like..." When asked to describe a situation, you're likely to hear how they felt about it, rather than particular concrete details.

When the feelings of inferiority hit the Four as a result of envy, that may come through in speech as putting themselves down—"I'm a terrible artist, it's no wonder no one buys my paintings"—or it may flip into a sense of superiority to escape the feeling of inferiority—"I can't believe she likes that film. It's such commercial garbage." Their go-to insult, because it's the worst thing anyone can be to a Four, is to call someone a "phony" or some variation of that, stemming from their value of authenticity.

As part of the Heart Center, the Four's language tends to include lots of emotional words and metaphors. They appreciate symbolism and often find it expresses their emotions more accurately than literal language. It wouldn't be uncommon to hear them compare their emotional state to something like a cloud, fungi, a jackrabbit, etc.

STEREOTYPES

The Four may be the most stereotyped of the Enneagram. In imagining a Four, one might picture a teenager with copious eyeliner who spends their time in class drawing anime and whose locker is plastered with band pictures of Evanescence and My Chemical Romance (I'm dating myself here, I know). Or maybe one imagines Virginia Woolf writing the scene in *To the Lighthouse* that describes the fruit on the table at a dinner party with such great detail and significance that it makes the reader's eyes glaze over. While, yes, this can be *part* of the Four, they tend to fly under the radar in everyday life by adjusting to societal norms ... somewhat.

Some Fours work in accounting. They may be your put-together therapist, your best friend who always listens without judgment, or your neighbor who grows the most beautiful sunflowers each year. No matter how much they learn to "fit in," they will always be deeply emotional and see the world a little differently from everyone else. Many of them learn to appear more like thinkers than feelers (those with a Five as their strongest wing), and many are quite ambitious in their dreams (those with a Three as their strongest wing).

There's a stereotype that Fours lack emotional fortitude and are overly sensitive. This can be the case for those who lack the self-awareness to understand that their emotions aren't truth. But for those who've learned the basics of observing their emotions rather than identifying with them, they can become a lighthouse that guides others through turbulent emotional waters, reminding them that all is not lost.

EASY MISTAKES TO MAKE

Fours are sometimes written like Sixes, in that their dialogue focuses on the negative, except (for Sixes) the negative they talk about is one that *could* happen in the future, the worst-case scenario. While Fours could linger on imagined future unhappiness, their attention is more likely to focus on what is *currently* misery-invoking or what's made them unhappy *in the past*.

Fours will tell stories of their misfortunes, missed opportunities, or victimizations to help explain their present emotional state, but they rarely look toward the future for more potential misery. The Six, meanwhile, keeps an eye on the future at all times to watch out for what misery might be coming down the pipeline. When a Four says, "We're all going to die," it might be with a sense of resignation or even relief. When a Six says, "We're all going to die," it's usually a warning. Both types are often told they're overreacting, though.

Any Four will tell you that they don't always live in their dark and moody emotions and that they do feel intensely overwhelmed by joy and beauty from time to time. They are emotionally sensitive, yes, but is that always a bad thing in an insensitive world?

EXAMPLES

Jane Eyre, Arwen (Lord of the Rings movies), Moira Rose (*Schitt's Creek*), Luna Lovegood (Harry Potter), Holden Caulfield (*The Catcher in the Rye*), Eeyore, Elio Perlman (*Call Me By Your Name*), Hades (Greek mythology), Erik "The Phantom" (*Phantom of the Opera*)

DEEP DIVE: ELIO PERLMAN

Deciding on the Four to dive into was the trickiest part of the deep dives. That's because it's unusual to have a Four character who's given the depth a Four deserves. It can be easy to simply write a character as weirdo or an outcast and assume you've written a Four (sorry, Fours, but this can't be news to you). As any Four will tell you, it's not that simple. Some people are outcasts by circumstance, some people are weird but not Fours, and some Fours learn to blend in … mostly.

One of the central concerns of the Four is understanding their inner world, who they are, and what it means to be living as their authentic self. While everyone goes through a "finding yourself" process in your teens and early twenties (and maybe later on, as life compels), there is one coming-of-age tale that stands out to me as quintessentially Four, and that's the novel Call Me By Your Name. *Not only is the narrator, Elio Perlman, seventeen years old for the majority of the novel, but he's also trying to understand his bisexuality as an ex-pat in Italy in the 1980s. Each of these individual elements made me put on my skeptic's hat when starting my close read, keeping an eye on the question of "Is he just an angsty bisexual teen but not a Four?" I got my answer on page one, and it didn't waver through the final sentence of the novel.*

The focus of this story on Elio's first homosexual relationship might not be as much a consequence of it being a coming-of-age moment but rather a reflection of the impact it had on his sense of identity throughout his entire life. In fact, we see how this short-lived affair echoes through his life long after the object of his obsession has left Italy.

That's why I chose Elio as my Four. The narrator speaks about his past from the perspective of adulthood—this whole book being the kind of nostalgia Fours enjoy—reflecting on the crisis of identity that he experienced one summer when he was seventeen years old and that shaped him for the rest of his life.

Analysis: When we first meet Elio, we don't actually meet him. Instead, we see the object of his obsession, Oliver, through his eyes. Elio is fixated on the American graduate student's use of the casual departing word "later," and all of the meaning that (Elio assumes) is packed into that. This is our first taste of Elio's tendency to jam meaning into every centimeter of space that he inhabits with his professor father's summer guest, twenty-four-year-old Oliver.

Fours are considered the meaning makers of the Enneagram, turning ordinary facts into symbols of something transcendent, weaving stories behind the minutiae of everyday life. We experience this from Elio on page one, and every subsequent page, as he tries to decode each gesture, facial expression, and word of his family's guest, whom he immediately becomes infatuated with. The word "later" itself becomes a stand-in symbol for Oliver throughout the narrative, a promise of something down the road that never quite culminates.

Elio and Oliver's friendship starts off with a pattern of heavy, lingering silence between them. From Elio's perspective, what's *unsaid* is the most crucial component of their interactions. Most of their conversations are high-brow, a sword fight of intellect about classical music and the great Western philosophers. It's a sparring for superiority that Fours often engage in when attracted to someone else. In Elio's case, he idolizes Oliver and wants nothing more than to be noticed by him, to be picked out, chosen as special, which demonstrates the Four's core desire to have significance. But more than that, Elio begins to stake his sense of identity on his relationship with Oliver. Every move Oliver makes around him means something and carries a sense of life-or-death importance for Elio. He exhibits a typical Type 4 desire to be seen without needing to ask for it during an early interaction with Oliver:

> "*What did one do around here?*" [asks Oliver]
>
> "*Nothing. Wait around for summer to end.*" [Elio replies]
>
> "*What did one do in the winter, then?*"
>
> *I smiled at the answer I was about to give. He got the gist and said, "Don't tell me. Wait for the summer to come, right?" I liked having my mind read.*

This is the kind of intensity of attention that Fours crave without daring to ask for it. To be seen deeply, to have one's "mind read," is a thrill for those who feel constantly misunderstood and strive to be special.

Elio seems to have found someone who sees him in a way that reaffirms he exists, and because of that, he develops a yearning for the houseguest that consumes him completely. His obsession occasionally leads to imitation, as he sees in Oliver both things that Elio has kept hidden, like his desire for another man, and things he feels he lacks, like confidence and charisma. We can see this blend of admiration and envy when he says: "I'd never heard someone his [Oliver's] age say, 'I know myself.' It intimidated me." Elio is just starting to know himself and begins to suspect that he can only know himself better through Oliver knowing him intimately.

Like most Fours, Elio's sense that he's lacking something someone else has leads to a kind of erotic envy that leaves him unmoored. He wonders, *Did I want to be like him? Did I want to be him? Or did I just want to have him?* He can never be sure, but he suspects the answer would become obvious if only he could have the sexual experience he's longing for.

In the meantime, Elio gratifies himself with fantasy. It's clear from his description of Oliver that he's stopped seeing a flawed person and begun envisioning him as a symbol for something else; this is a common pattern of Fours, who would rather engage with a perfect fantasy than accept the mundanity of reality. But it's also an objectifying pattern, which Elio doesn't seem to mind, even finds more erotic. He objectifies the idea of Oliver in all kinds of ways, including imagining an apricot as Oliver's ass, a symbol that takes the form of a peach later and becomes not only a stand-in for Elio's craving for the older man but also for uncontained lust and erotic yearnings in a broader sense.

Elio's approach to getting what he wants, in this case Oliver, is to withdraw. He plays coy, flirting in imperceptible ways that he imagines Oliver can read. He tries to appear unaffected, not particularly comfortable with the part of himself that likes men along with women. To get the attention he wants, he withdraws; a hallmark of the Four.

What he withdraws to are fantasies no one can take from him. He doesn't trust that he'll get what he wants from the outside world, so he provides it to himself in this way. He creates an idealization of what it would be like to have sex with Oliver that contains the man in the throes of passion saying, "You'll kill me if you stop." There's a threat of devastation, of being dashed upon rocky Mediterranean shores, that haunts Elio's erotic needs. And he loves it.

When the two finally do sneak away to be alone, after Elio has decided he'd rather die than say nothing to Oliver about his feelings, they finally share their first kiss. Elio finds himself disappointed by the reality of the interaction he's fantasized about repeatedly, a suffering Fours experience over and over again in their life (and that a Four author might experience when trying to pull the perfect fantasy version of the story into reality, only to feel like it's missing something integral that damns it to mediocrity).

The *majority* of this novel takes place in Elio's imagination; pages are filled with the heavy meanings he reads into everything, the fantasies he concocts, the assumptions he clings to like, "I knew he knew I knew" that he takes to be hard truth.

When he finally does get his wish and can experience the sexual intimacy he craves with Oliver, it becomes clearer than ever that Elio's hope in this intimacy is not to know *Oliver* better, but to know *himself* better through Oliver—a Four's quest for self-knowledge knows no bounds.

He tells Oliver, "You'll kill me if you stop," to prompt Oliver to say the same to him, manifesting his long-held fantasy into reality. The encounter culminates with Oliver, who seems to understand exactly what Elio needs from this interaction, telling Elio to call his *own* name when he climaxes. They each call the other by their own name, sealing something mystical and sacred between them, knowing themselves forevermore through having known the other.

Their affair continues on in secret through the summer, including a trip to Rome to meet with Oliver's literary agent and other aspiring writers who stay out late, drip in eroticism themselves, and provide a version of adulthood that Elio knows isn't real and doesn't need to be real. The fantasy is enough. His summer with Oliver is enough. Because though it leaves him wanting and craving, getting more of Oliver—having continued access to him—would mean that there was no space for longing and no opportunity for nostalgia as the years pass, both things that are precious and give meaning to the relationship. Elio (and most Fours) value those feelings beyond what's "real" and "everyday."

Once Oliver leaves Italy, returning to the States, Elio catches himself lying miserably in bed one day, trying to dull the pain. With a jolt, he realizes that dulling the pain also dulls the memory of that summer, and so he resolves himself to hold on to the sting of loss so that he can hold on to the memory. In this way, we see the Four's tendency to embrace pain as a way of grasping at the past itself, and we understand now on a deeper level why this happens. Even at seventeen, Elio knows instinctively that some things are sweeter once they have ended and all that's left is the longing and nostalgia.

While Elio does encounter Oliver a couple of times years *later*, he seems to understand that trying to reignite what they had before would only muddle the passionate memory and taint its potency, rather than amplify it.

In many ways, the story of that summer is the only true story Elio knows of himself, so he protects it. And in their final meeting, his yearning for Oliver is still present, and he longs to call his own name in ecstasy, just one more time, to return to that moment where he finally knew himself intimately through Oliver.

THE THINKING CENTER

TYPE 5

TYPE NAMES

The Investigator, the Quiet Specialist, the Perspective of Wisdom, the Observer, the Specialist, the Expert

CORE MOTIVATIONS

Fear: of being incapable or incompetent

Desire: to be capable and competent

The Five's core motivations often take the form of gathering knowledge and trying to understand the world around them.

BRIEF DESCRIPTION

Fives are focused on how the world works. They want to understand the mechanics and underlying logic of things, whether it be people, nature, or their particular occupation. The Five has a thirst for knowledge because *only when they know enough* will they feel safe. The Five doesn't like being in situations where they feel incompetent or don't know exactly how things work. Underlying this anxiety is the fear that they will not have the necessary mental, emotional, and physical resources to handle what might come their way.

Fives do not like the idea of being dependent on others for resources, mostly because they see other people as a possible drain on their battery. Their energy is a resource they spend a lot of time monitoring and guarding, and as a result, they're usually the first to withdraw from social situations, earning them a reputation as a hermit or even as antisocial.

Fives attempt to create safety by observing the world rather than living in it. This tendency toward conceptualizing, however, often leads to them being wrong in their predictions. The world is not as neatly organized as the Five may hope, and only through gathering experiential data can they start to understand that.

Yet this same tendency to prefer theory over experience also results in one of the Five's greatest contributions to the world: creating simple and elegant solutions. Because Fives tend to live firmly in their thinking centers, disconnecting from both their emotions and physical sensations, they like to take the complex and boil it down to something simple, like $E = mc^2$, for instance.

While Fives tend to imagine themselves as objective observers, that can never truly be the case. Even though they lose connection to their emotions, those emotions still exist inside of them, influencing their thinking in ways they might not be aware of. This can lead the Five to call emotional impulses logical conclusions. If the Five isn't careful, they may start with a conclusion that makes them feel safe and superior and then seek out only the information that backs it up—the exact opposite of science.

The Five's lifelong inner battle is between their need to know and their ability to learn. When the core fear of the Five is triggered, they may respond by needing to *already* know something and will grab the nearest conclusion and double down on it. The fear of not knowing may be too great to tolerate. Only when the Five admits they do not know can the process of learning begin, and only when they step outside of the fear of being incompetent in the present can the liberated energy of genuine curiosity emerge and lead to breakthroughs for the future.

A Five who cannot learn to sit with the discomfort of feeling incompetent or incapable is a Five who cannot continue learning. When this happens, the Five may opt for making other people look foolish by trolling or antagonizing them, causing others to flare up with emotions while the Five remains smugly emotionless, using that as further proof that they hold the intellectually superior position.

Once a Five can learn that feeling foolish is optional and being wrong is a necessary part of the process for reaching a sound conclusion, they're able to take risks that allow for greater understanding and can remain comfortable and happy despite there being things they still don't understand in the world around them. Knowledge becomes an exciting quest rather than cumbersome armor.

WINGS

5w4

The Four wing will pull the Five's attention not just toward thoughts but also toward emotions, though they are less likely to feel their feelings than to think about them. The access to their Feeling Center allows Fives to better express themselves and create deeper relationships with others ... though possibly not many others, as the Five's tendency to withdraw into their head is compounded by the Four's tendency to withdraw into their feelings. The wing builds deeper connections, but it also tends to push this type toward introversion.

The Four wing helps pull the Five toward the heart, allowing ideas and understanding of the world to be informed not only by facts, but by emotional data, which offers the Five a fuller understanding of humanity.

5w6

While the Six wing can encourage a Five to think more in terms of group resources and show courage in stating their opinions, it can also draw them into cynicism that casts an unearned suspicion on those around them, causing the Five to isolate from others more than they might have already. If the Six's pattern of doubt creeps in, it will compound the Five's need for intellectual certainty, which can leave the 5w6 feeling panicked, angry, and misanthropic. If the Five is healthier, though, this pattern of doubt can keep the Five open to new ideas rather than getting entrenched in outdated ones in a need to feel certain.

The Six wing means the Five is solidly planted in the Thinking Center. Without learning to access information from the other two centers, they are likely to bounce back and forth between doubt and certainty, relying too much on observation and conceptualizing and not enough on emotions and lived experience.

LEVELS OF DEVELOPMENT

Healthy: Visionary, open-minded, finds fresh ways to view the world, possesses extreme perceptiveness and insight, curious and eager to learn, participant in their life rather than observer, focused and easily engrossed in a subject, strong skills of prediction.

Average: Leans heavily on conceptualizing, insists on preparing ideas completely before sharing them with others, more concerned with their own views and interpretations than reality, detaches and compartmentalizes knowledge, antagonistic to protect inner world, becomes a provocateur instead of an innovator, takes up extreme or radical views.

Unhealthy: Retreats into isolation, adopts a nihilistic view of reality, need to know ferments into a focus on the arcane or a disturbing reality no one else understands, obsessed with threatening ideas, horrified of the world, prone to a psychotic break from reality and self-destruction.

VICE

The Five's vice is **Avarice**. Sensing their isolation and separateness from others, Fives strive to be self-sufficient, and they do that through holding on tight to the resources they possess. They don't trust that what they need will find them, and they fear that the world will take from them whatever isn't locked down. This results in a pattern of stinginess that only increases their sense of isolation and separateness.

Your Type 5 character will get themselves into trouble by closing themselves off from the information and resources others have to offer. They may even close themselves off from the information their own emotions and body are sending them, as means of staying separate from others and the demands of the outside world.

VIRTUE

The virtue of the Five is **Non-Attachment**. Only once the Five can stop clinging to their resources and be open to the idea that what is meant for them will find them can they experience a state of Non-Attachment. This doesn't look like isolation or *detachment*, but rather it's a deep appreciation for what exists while understanding that everything is meant to circulate throughout the world—this includes energy, money, knowledge, and other resources.

STRESS TYPE

Moves toward Seven. When the Five's quest to understand the world leads to a dead end or answers that they later discover are incorrect, the Five's focus on depth might fracture as they grope around for something—anything—to hold on to. They take on some of the Seven's hopping attentional patterns and may begin to act frantically or hyperactively. Their desire not to look foolish can make it too risky to focus deeply on a single topic or project, and they spread themselves over many instead, without gaining much understanding on any particular topic.

If the Five can take this rare opportunity to experience breadth over depth as a way to explore ideas and beliefs contrary to their own, they avoid getting locked into one way of thinking and can find something truer and more lasting to build upon. Rather than needing everything to fit their theory, the break from their dominant type allows them to adapt their theory to fit the facts.

GROWTH TYPE

As the Five lets go of their fear of being depleted and learn to trust that the outside world offers energy to those who engage with it, they move toward their growth type of Eight. They accept that some things cannot be understood through the head alone and must be experienced by the body and through taking action before confidence in the outcome emerges.

COMMON THEME PAIRINGS

Truth, reality, avarice, memory, exploration, respect, interdependence, resources, knowledge, isolation, abundance/scarcity

TRIAD/CENTER

Head/Thinking/Cognitive

Fives are the most obviously Head Center type of this triad. They spend most of their time in their mind, thinking and processing new information internally rather than needing to process it externally with others. Fives lose connection with their other two centers from overusing their head, and as a result, they overuse their Head Center even more, thinking about emotions instead of feeling them and observing the world instead of interacting with it. If you ask a Five how they feel, they'll often tell you what they think.

The problem with being so firmly planted in only one of the centers is that the Five is missing out on two-thirds of the information they could gain about the world around them. There is important information to be gained from feeling feelings and tuning into intuition and bodily sensations, but the Five tends to not value this as much (or at all) compared with the information they gain from thinking, observing, and reading. Unfortunately, the answers they're looking for cannot be gained without first reconnecting with their heart and body. Whatever "elegant solution" they come up with in the theoretical may turn out to be garbage in the experimental because they've overlooked important human elements.

Anxiety/Scarcity/Security

Fives want to gather resources to themselves to avoid needing to rely on others. Relationships can be a fraught topic for Fives, since they struggle to connect to their own emotions and therefore feel drained and sometimes confused by others' emotional needs. One of the ways Fives cope with this is to hoard resources. They chase a feeling of certainty that they'll have what they need when they need it by collecting it for themselves.

Sometimes the focus can be on material resources like money and food, but often it's the intangible resource of knowledge (frequently taking on the material form of books). The Five struggles to remember that there is a natural flow to resources when we stay connected to others through friendship or community, but we can't tap into those resources as needed when we're as self-isolating as the Five tends to be. They forget that you don't have to store a lifetime supply of apples if you have a friend with an apple tree.

This anxiety around resources and security can manifest into displays of greed or avarice, with the Five feeling like they can never possibly have enough to ensure they're set. This anxiety can lead to a need for certainty that can never be achieved, causing the Five to seek more knowledge and understanding, but in the least risky way possible so as to avoid feeling foolish.

INTERACTION STYLE

Fives are a **withdrawn** type. They don't trust that the world will offer up the security they need, so they withdraw and provide it for themselves. This means they enjoy gathering resources to themselves, like knowledge or physical collections, not trusting that the resources they need will find them in any other way. This shows up in their need for privacy and a leaning toward isolation.

DIALOGUE

Because Fives are speaking from their Head Center, their dialogue will use "it seems" and "I think" rather than "I feel like." You may even throw in some "Well, actually …" Fives aren't known to be talkers unless they believe they have useful information to contribute, and they tend to stick to the facts.

Fives often speak in a presentational or lecture-like manner, laying out their knowledge for others in a factual way, almost as an offering. This is a contribution given to those whom they believe will respect the information by using it or at least believing it. When Fives are around those who they *don't* believe will appreciate the information they have to offer, or, god forbid, will ridicule them for offering it, they're likely to sit on it, even if it could help the situation.

It's rare to hear a Five speak from their own experience unless they're mentioning a credential that qualifies them as an expert, as in "As someone who spent twenty years researching this ..." followed by facts. Because the Five likes to think of themselves as an objective observer of life, they prefer to speak from a position of consensus. This may look like presenting their personal observations as a universal truth. Rather than "I think it would work better if..." they might say, "It works better when..."

STEREOTYPES

The Five is often viewed as the hermit, the genius, and somewhat antisocial on the whole. This is a result of their tendency to withdraw to protect their resources like time and energy, and it's certainly a true part of the Five (not all of them are geniuses, but they do all like to think deeply, which can produce certain insights).

But Fives can also enjoy the company of others and be social people, so long as the social situation is one that doesn't require too much of them emotionally and focuses on topics and conversations that they find mentally stimulating. Fives tend to have a few close friendships, and so long as no one expects them to engage daily and understands there will be times the Five needs time alone in their cave, Fives make incredibly trustworthy friends. Their tendency to hold on to information and their own preference for privacy allows them to be vaults for the things their close friends share with them.

While Fives are frequently stereotyped as intellectuals or snobs, there are also Fives who go hard in the other direction, eschewing traditional understandings of the world and digging into the fringe of understanding, like the paranormal, for instance. The Five's desire to know things that others don't ("secret knowledge") can often lead them to conspiratorial thinking, too, if they fail to acknowledge the emotional needs that are governing their thirst for not only avoiding feeling foolish, but feeling like the only one who *isn't* being fooled.

EASY MISTAKES TO MAKE

Fives aren't robots. They still have emotional lives and a physical body. They still have intuition, even if they aren't always attuned to it. They can be emotionally sensitive and generous and offer their knowledge as a way of reaching out and soothing others. Yes, facts can be soothing, especially to those swirling in emotions. Facts can lead to perspective or a solution to the current problem. While Fives tend to express themselves from the Head Center, emotions are still coloring their perspective, as is the case with every type.

The Venn diagram between Fives and those on the autism spectrum is not a perfect circle, so it's important not to convolute the two as you write. Yes, some Fives are on the spectrum. But so are some people of every type. If you'd like to write a character on the spectrum, great, but don't simply write them like a Five by default. (Yes, I get this question *a lot*.)

EXAMPLES

Sherlock Holmes, Belle (Disney's *Beauty and the Beast*), Mr. Spock (Star Trek), Holly Gibney (various Stephen King novels), Velma Dinkley (*Scooby Doo*), Walter White (*Breaking Bad*), Severus Snape (Harry Potter), Hannibal Lecter (*The Silence of the Lambs*).

DEEP DIVE: HOLLY GIBNEY

It only seemed appropriate to select a Five character who was an actual investigator for this deep dive. Sherlock Holmes, in his many incarnations, seemed like low-hanging fruit, so instead I selected one of my favorite investigators in modern fiction: Stephen King's Holly Gibney.

Holly appears in multiple King novels, particularly those that follow the investigations of retired cop Bill Hodges. Having read some of the books where she appears, I realized that my favorite version of her is actually the one in the HBO adaptation of The Outsider. *There are marked differences between the way Holly is written in this version as opposed to the books, the least of which is her race (she's described as white in the books, but she's Black in the show). In the ten-episode TV series, as opposed to the books, Holly has more than simply a stellar memory. Instead, she knows things she has no reason to know —a supernatural ability that ultimately helps her do what needs to be done to identify the dark force behind multiple brutal child slayings.*

The Outsider includes all the trigger warnings you'd expect from a Stephen King tale, and it explores the agonizing and devastating pain of grief. I hesitated before including it for that reason, but ultimately it felt important to use an example from the horror genre to show how much it can benefit when the depth of the Enneagram is applied to its characters. I won't lie and say there weren't some heart-stopping, jaw-dropping, "holy fuck" moments in this show, but hey, sometimes it's just nice to feel something, right?

Analysis: When we first meet Holly Gibney (ep. 3), she's staring out her apartment window, reciting obscure facts about various makes and models of cars. It's clear she lives alone and without much fuss about décor. She walks to the pub below her apartment and stops in her tracks. "You're in my seat," she tells an unsuspecting man at the bar. He's caught off guard but ultimately vacates it, presumably preferring to let the weirdo have her way than start an altercation. Holly is clearly a loner with a desire for routine and a head full of statistics. She shows almost no visible reaction to anything and clings to her obscure knowledge like a superstition. She is, in short, clearly a Head Center type.

As with most Fives, there's no small talk with Holly. She cuts straight to the point. While she doesn't appreciate how everyone makes jokes and chitchats, she's able to observe it closely and understand it to an extent.

In the context of this mystery, Holly serves as a foil for the highly skeptical Detective Ralph Anderson, the protagonist. He finds himself in a clusterfuck of a case when the body of a local child is found in the woods, torn up something terrible. Multiple witnesses claim they saw local English teacher and likeable dad Terry Maitland covered in blood, leaving the scene. Det. Anderson has gathered multiple angles of CCTV that show Terry moving around town that day, after the slaying. Terry's DNA and fingerprints are even found on the victim's body and in the white van that's covered in the victim's blood. It seems like a slam-dunk case, so much so that Det. Anderson orders Terry be arrested in the middle of the Little League game he's coaching, putting on a show for the whole town.

Only one problem: video footage from a teacher conference seventy miles away seems to prove that Terry Maitland was *there* during the time of the murder. Det. Anderson, himself a grieving father, cannot make sense of how the killer *must* be Terry Maitland even while it *can't* be Terry Maitland, so he's facing an impossible situation for a staunch skeptic like him who relies on hard facts to feel safe and supported in reality.

At the recommendation of a friend, Det. Anderson allows private investigator Holly Gibney to help out with the investigation, despite having been taken off the case after a shooting in the line of duty. The two characters create a potent polarity in their understanding of knowledge. Det. Anderson is stuck because the facts don't fit his preexisting understanding of the world—namely, that a man cannot be in two places at once.

Holly, meanwhile, who has a *strong* Four wing that allows her to tolerate the unknown and unknowable in a way that Fives usually struggle with, is able to approach the situation from a position of allowing the facts to *expand* her understanding of reality until they make some kind of sense.

While the Five often tries to soothe their core fear of being incompetent or incapable through learning, the Four understands that the world is complicated, complex, and mysterious and has more of a tolerance for that. Holly allows her wing to help offset her core fear in this way.

This shows a degree of health that most Fives struggle to achieve but that we see in great thinkers like Stephen Hawking, who are able to reach beyond what we know to create theories in which the unexplainable might be understood.

During her first meeting with Det. Anderson, he says, "I don't have any tolerance for the unexplainable," to which Holly replies, "Well then, sir, you'll have no tolerance for me."

The reason Holly is able to access this open thinking ability is due, in large part, to the mystery of her own abilities and a childhood where she was poked and prodded by doctors and scientists to understand how she was able to know things she had no reason to know. It's in her sharing this biographic information (as facts, with no emotions attached) with Det. Anderson upon their first meeting that he offers her compassion for her parents putting her through that. This small gesture, while the emotion of it makes Holly visibly uncomfortable in the moment, creates a bond between them as Det. Anderson (probably a 6w5) becomes an advocate for her when she needs it, and Holly doesn't give up on Det. Anderson when the theory of the case she produces extends far beyond what he's willing to believe exists in this world.

At one point, early in her investigation and before she presents her out-there theory, she calls Det. Anderson to give him a tidbit. "I know I could've waited until I had more information ... It's just sometimes, every once in a while, I like to hear the voice of someone who's on my side." The Loyal Skeptic (Six) finds something important in the Loner Investigator (Five).

He even asks her, "Where are you going with all this?" to which she replies, "Wherever it takes me," showing that she's following the facts to whatever new understanding they may lead her, not trying to fit them to her worldview to feel safe and on solid ground.

In short, Holly doesn't get caught in the typical trap Fives fall into of *already needing to know* that can keep them from learning and understanding new things. She knows there are unexplainable things in this world, because she is one.

What makes Holly a particularly interesting Five is her religiosity. She carries a protective talisman, showing off that Four wing, and believes in God, which is unusual to see with a cerebral Five character. However, she believes in God the way you would expect her type to: "He's the explanation ... for, uh, everything in this world that ever happened to me that I don't understand; that I never will." For her, God is the absence of what she knows, which is admittedly very little. God is all the things she has yet to discover, so in that way, through God, all things *are* possible. Maybe just not in the way most people mean that. God plays a central and healthy role in keeping her feeling safe despite not understanding certain important goings on. Fives usually *only* feel safe when they understand. She's found a workaround for herself through her religion.

Holly is a private person, not interested in sharing about herself but committed to sharing the truth as she sees it, which is a hallmark of Fives. She even says, "If I believe something to be true, then I have to deliver that truth no matter what." And she does, when she presents her theory of the murders to Det. Anderson and the rest of their ragtag group investigating the crimes. While most of her natural speech pattern is presentational, we see that talk style come through especially clearly during her monotone presentation of what is a sensational and supernatural conclusion about their suspect.

Det. Anderson, who, up to that point, has put his trust in her, feels betrayed and blindsided by what he sees as an unbelievable theory of some sort of paranormal being behind multiple child murders. This is a severing point in their relationship, and he stops going to bat for her. But some in the group aren't as skeptical as Det. Anderson and believe Holly's onto something, allowing her to stay in the conversation—and this continues to serve as a challenge to Det. Anderson to allow the evidence to put a crack in his narrow version of the world.

As Holly tries to disabuse Det. Anderson of his limited idea of what is and could be, she threatens to disrupt his grieving process for his young son, who died the year before. You can sense that in holding on to his idea of how the world is, he's holding on to the world in which his son once existed. When he's feeling the most lost and unmoored by the investigation's unexplainable nature, we find him sleeping on his son's bed in a room that's been untouched and preserved.

At the urging of his wife, who's concerned that denying the reality of what he's up against may get him killed by it, Det. Anderson tries to believe in Holly's far-fetched theory, and in beginning to entertain it, he's finally able to break through and accept evidence that seems to confirm her claims as true.

Holly's curiosity overrides her fear of the unknown, and only through that process is she able to guide the protagonist toward what he needs: to accept that there are some things he may never understand, things that exist but do not fit neatly in his understanding of the world that he once inhabited with his son.

Once the investigation has concluded and Holly is about to depart, Det. Anderson inquires how she was able to do it, how she was able to believe her own freaky theory. She replies, "An outsider knows an outsider." Through the self-knowledge and uniqueness of her strong Four wing, Holly's Five is able to access deeper knowledge of the world ... and deeper un-knowledge.

Before Holly leaves, Det. Anderson asks her, with some obvious desperation, "What else is out there?" Holly, perhaps not wanting to spoil the wonder and certainly comfortable with the mystery, only offers him a mischievous shrug before she departs. The lone observer, the (literally) private investigator, has allowed facts to lead her toward unveiling a part of her version of God. Through the process, she's also granted Det. Anderson the ability to believe in what he cannot see, so much so that when his wife suggests they may one day see their son again, he's able to accept the much-needed comfort of that idea. Maybe they will. Who knows?

TYPE 6

TYPE NAMES

The Loyalist, the Loyal Skeptic, the Guardian, the Troubleshooter, the Doubter, the True Believer

CORE MOTIVATIONS

Fear: of being without support or guidance

Desire: to have support or guidance

The Six's core motivations present themselves as seeking security and protection.

BRIEF DESCRIPTION

Sixes are attuned to safety, security, and support. They look skeptically at the underlying motivations of others, trying to guess at what's not being said and often landing on the most cynical possibility when the motivations are obscure. Sixes are a tricky type to pin down because they have a split within their ranks—phobic and counterphobic. This means that in the face of uncertainty and doubt, the Six might take the *phobic* approach by running away from the threat, being stuck in doubt, or even seeking an external authority figure to save them from the danger. Or they may take the *counterphobic* approach when they sense uncertainty and doubt, which looks like recklessness or rebellion against perceived authority.

The central tension of the Six is that they've stopped trusting their inner authority. That little voice that nudges many of the other types toward the next right thing feels either absent to the Six, or they've learned not to trust it when they do hear it. This creates a familiar feeling of self-doubt, which causes the Six to seek external assurances of security in the form of advice, guidance, or protection. (Sometimes this becomes seeking advice from too many people and not having an effective internal anchor to decide between contradicting perspectives, which leads to even more doubt.)

Because of the Six's attunement to security, they make excellent risk assessors. They're usually the first to see the trouble up ahead, and as a result, they frequently end up the Cassandra at their workplace or in their friend group, always predicting the danger and rarely being believed. They may not be right all the time—after all, not every worst-case scenario comes to pass—but they're right enough that it keeps their attention focused on future problems. This focus on impending disaster can understandably make it difficult for a Six to relax, no matter how many people tell them to. To a Six, nobody else seems properly alert or prepared.

Authority is a constant tension in the life of a Six. On the one hand, a protective authority figure who can tell them what to do when their doubt kicks in has a certain soothing appeal. This "authority" may look like a teacher, parent, religious leader, trusted friend, politician, or sometimes even a guru (read: cult leader). In that way, Sixes may be particularly prone to authoritarian thinking when their fear kicks up.

On the other hand (and sometimes at the same time!), the Six can remain mistrustful of and rebellious toward authority, sensing that someone in that position is a general security threat if they choose to be. This paradox may manifest like rallying behind a charismatic political leader (authoritarian) but mistrusting "the government" (mistrust of authority). It may also be as simple as trusting a friend they consider to be someone of authority but also keeping that friend under a watchful eye, testing them in small ways for signs of betrayal ... and what we look for, we typically find (whether we must exaggerate reality or not).

When the Six begins to reconnect with their gut and their Inner Authority, the insecurity and anxiety in their life begins to lessen. They don't have to spend so much time predicting what bad things might happen because they remember that they are actually quite good in a crisis situation. They tend to know what to do or whom to ask for help. Maybe they didn't as a child, but as a result of that, they've spent their adult life refining the skill.

They begin to trust themselves, including trusting that they will know what to do when the time comes, rather than needing to rehearse their next imagined catastrophe on a loop. This sense of grounding and trust in self allows them to remain loyal and reliable friends, as they stop projecting their fears onto others and can begin offering the generous assumptions necessary for strong, long-term friendship.

This is when Sixes really shine. They become the glue that holds groups of people together, showing up for their friends and allies at a moment's notice and without questions or judgment. They also become an inspiration to others with their courage. After all, if you're not *afraid* while you act, it's not a courageous act, so who has more potential for daily courageous acts than the type that sees the world in terms of danger and safety?

WINGS

6w5

The Five wing may help the Six slow down and take a step back to observe their fear when it sets in rather than letting it pick up steam. The Five can be the steady voice talking them through the physical anxiety response. Then again, it can also become fuel for the anxiety, if its need for certainty isn't kept under close observation. The Five's tendency to hoard may be used to support the Six's need for security, which doesn't scratch the itch so much as aggravate it. Often the antidote for anxiety is purposeful action, but a strong Five wing is likely to discourage that first step, pulling the Six toward withdrawing into themselves until they think themselves to a point of certainty on an outcome (which may never arrive and is a flawed goal anyway).

The Five wing is likely to keep the Six more introverted and less willing to share their anxieties and concerns with others. Since speaking our fear to someone we trust can often be the best way to overcome the anxiety, this tendency toward not doing so can leave the Six in a doubt loop that builds until it explodes in reckless or desperate action.

6w7

The Seven wing may add a touch of playfulness and optimism to the Six that helps them deal with the unknown. These Sixes tend to be more self-deprecating and better able to imagine good things happening in the future rather than only seeing the possible pitfalls and dangers. At the same time, the Seven's pattern of scattered attention may also influence the Six by creating disorganized thinking that draws them further away from an actionable solution and more toward attempting to flee the problem altogether.

The Seven wing is likely to make the Six more extroverted and engaged with the world around them. It also makes them slightly less likely to stick with a relationship when the going gets tough, challenging the Six's natural tendency toward loyalty.

LEVELS OF DEVELOPMENT

Healthy: Trusting of self and others, courageous, highly cooperative while maintaining independence, can imagine what might go right, not afraid to lead, forms strong relationships with others, shows deep support for movements and individuals they care about, naturally builds and fosters healthy communities that create stability and security for others.

Average: Bases decisions on safest option rather than most impactful or courageous, seeks security through alliances, seeks protective external authority, functions in a state of hypervigilance, indecisive and anxious, begins sorting people into allies and enemies, approaches novelty with suspicion, prone to authoritarian beliefs, projects undesired parts of self onto others.

Unhealthy: Suspicion turns to paranoia, volatile as they vacillate between flight and flight, adopts radical beliefs to find footing and security, feelings of persecution or that everyone is out to get them validate their urge to lash out, can become hysterical and turn to self-destructive numbing behaviors, can justify backstabbing as they imagine betrayal everywhere.

VICE

The Six's vice is **Doubt**. This presents as hypervigilance and a desperate need for certainty related to their safety and support from others. This is not healthy skepticism. They want assurance that they can relax, while also worrying that relaxing is the best way to end up a target. This certainty seeking (while also mistrusting anything claiming to be certainty) leaves the Six doubting their relationships, their decisions, and, especially, their inner voice. They may become stuck in a pattern of doubt, spinning their wheels, or they may learn to act immediately and without much thought as soon as the pattern tickles their brain.

Your Type 6 will get themselves into trouble by second-guessing everything and failing to act when it's called for. They may also preemptively betray others who they suspect may betray them later.

VIRTUE

The virtue of the Six is **Courage**. Only once the Six can accept that their Doubt is not moving them closer to safety can they begin to loosen their grip on it and experience the state of Courage. By releasing their demand to feel certain about their safety before taking action, the Six can hear their inner authority's call when it's time to act *despite* their fear and doubt, to show up for and protect others.

STRESS TYPE

Moves toward Three. When the Six's attempts to create certainty and external security continue to fail, they may take on some of the "I'll do it myself" extreme productivity of the Three as well as a cutthroat approach to building security. They can start to slip out of their collaborative way of thinking and begin viewing survival as a zero-sum game. Not everyone can win, and they don't have any plans of losing.

If the Six uses this stress period as a moment of connecting with their internal ability to create security for themselves rather than waiting for outside assurances, they can return to a more collaborative approach to life where they don't need certainty that others will always have their backs, because they know they can provide for themselves if needed. This allows them to let their guard down and connect with the safety of the present moment.

GROWTH TYPE

As the Six stops living in future predictions and develops faith in their ability to know what to do in the moment, they are able to access some of the peace and calmness of their growth type, the Nine. When they learn that safety can only exist in the present, and that they have access to safety most of the time, they're better able to recognize when vigilance is appropriate to a situation versus when it's keeping them from embracing safety and connection.

COMMON THEME PAIRINGS

Loyalty, responsibility, trust, fear, authority, security, courage, abandonment, support, reliance

TRIAD/CENTER

Head/Thinking/Cognitive

When Sixes learn they're a Thinking Center type, they might reply, "Yeah, the Overthinking Center." Sixes spend a lot of time in their head conjuring up scenarios and rehearsing for possible trouble. The Six has a tendency to attempt to do the work of their gut (Body Center) with their Head Center. They try to think themselves to a degree of certainty about external security that may trigger action, but unfortunately what they're seeking doesn't exist.

This pattern is a result of losing touch with their Inner Authority. They hope that a clear path forward may appear in an obvious way through thinking only, and when two options seem roughly the same or hold similar threat levels, the Six gets caught in the pattern of doubt. Doubt is essentially the brain saying yes and no at the same time, and the Six can get stuck in this loop, hoping that one option will reveal itself to be clearly more of a sure thing than the others.

But without the Action Center's help, this pattern can compound without generating action. The Six will reach out for advice and support but might receive conflicting advice that further adds to the pattern of doubt, or they may poke holes in all the advice they receive rather than consider it. They may ultimately seek out a confident authority figure to do the decision-making for them. (The Six often assigns authority to whomever projects the most confidence, rather than whoever is the most knowledgeable or correct.)

Only once the Six learns to recognize the trap that doubt sets for them can they begin to view doubt as an indicator that they've collected all the information they can from thinking and predicting alone. The rest of the information can only be attained through action. What action? Any, really. The only way out of doubt is through action, and if the Six is waiting to stop feeling scared before taking the action, they may stay there forever. Courage and faith are the required antidotes.

Anxiety/Scarcity/Security

Because the natural flow of the Six's attention goes toward what could go wrong in the future, it's not a shocker that this type lives in a state of low-grade anxiety. Over time, the Six trains their nervous system to remain in a state of hypervigilance that only focused attention and mindfulness practices can begin to unwind. Specifically, the hypervigilance of the Six is directed toward whether the people around them can be trusted and are safe—or are they snakes?

This hypervigilance isn't just for themselves, though. The Six looks out for anyone they consider to be under their care, which may turn them into a catastrophizing boss or overbearing parent, always describing scenes of disaster that might occur if one lets one's guard down even for a second.

At the same time, this focus on security and preparation can make the Six a great friend to have around in a pinch, as they're not surprised by whatever trouble might appear and are probably ready to offer the support others need to handle it. While they may treat themselves to an "I told you so," the Six more than deserves that little treat with how much of a burden they assume for the safety and security of their group while others screw around and enjoy the perks of living with less anxiety.

INTERACTION STYLE

Sixes are a **compliant** type. They try to earn their security through service and duty to others. They feel like they must appease others, often a particular authority, to keep themselves safe and resourced.

DIALOGUE

The eye toward future possibilities (usually the ones a person would want to avoid) leads the Six to speak in cautionary ways. Their mind can jump to the repercussions of current actions, able to see the way present decisions echo into future consequences. That's often reflected in their speech through *if/then* sentences or trying to slow down the more action-centric around them to think for just one fucking second before acting. It also translates to a lot of "what if" questions that remain open ended. The Six will ask the question, but they won't necessarily follow it through to its conclusion, and if they do, they're unlikely to follow it through to a conclusion of rainbows and sunshine or far enough along to see a reality where bad stuff might happen but they are still okay.

If you imagine being in the mind of a Six, where danger is always a decision away, you can imagine that one of the Six's natural ways of coping is gallows humor. Indeed, Sixes are some of the funniest people to be around in a bad situation as a result of their patterns. Their sense of humor might be summed up with the sentences: "What's the worst that can happen? We all die horrendously? At least then we won't have to wonder what'll happen next." Sixes can be relied on to crack a joke in the face of danger as a pressure release, and they're not afraid to go dark with it. To them, death and disaster are nothing if not familiar presences, and the Six often feels strangely at home in dire situations. It's not uncommon for a Six to use this gallows humor as a bridge to cross the threshold from fear to courage.

STEREOTYPES

The Six is often imagined as the phobic, skittish, or twitchy type, and while this is sometimes true, it overlooks the counterphobic version, which all Sixes can slip into from time to time, that rushes *toward* risk. This is not necessarily in a brave way, but more in a reckless one. This counterphobic presentation can mean that the Six actually *starts* confrontation (having no tolerance for their doubt and preferring a bad but certain outcome to an uncertain future), rather than avoiding it.

Sixes aren't all fight-or-flight, either. They learn to put on a brave face and adapt as people show annoyance with their warnings. They may tend toward careers where one excels by learning and adhering to rules, like auditors or accountants, or where calculating risk is a large part of the work, like actuaries. But they also tend toward high-risk jobs with baked-in camaraderie and loyalty, like law enforcement and the military. So long as the Six doesn't lose all trust in the authority positioned above them, these jobs can suit their attentional patterns, core fear, and dark humor well.

EASY MISTAKES TO MAKE

The behavior of the counterphobic Six can look a hell of a lot like that of an Eight. Because of this, writers will tend toward simply making every bold and courageous character an Eight with the accompanying core fear of being harmed and controlled, rather than doing something more nuanced and choosing to write a counterphobic Six, with their core fear of being without support and guidance. Sometimes the author will even switch back and forth between these types without realizing it, and the result is a passage that feels slightly "off" to the reader.

The social responsibility and dutiful nature of the Six will sometimes cause authors to blend it with a One. However, Sixes don't function out of a sense of personal obligation so much as a desire to offer the loyalty and security to others that they hope to receive in return. This difference may be subtle and exist mostly below the surface, but it shows up in a big way at the character's major decision points. Will they do what's right or what will safeguard the support they've built for themselves? Are they more loyal to people (Sixes) or their principles (Ones)?

It's also easy to sideline Sixes to supporting roles, overlooking their potential to make strong protagonists or antagonists. Don't assume they're all sidekicks to more confident characters, though. They can also deliver the huge amounts of courage needed for a leading role … and a devious and devastating betrayal only a true villain could pull off.

EXAMPLES

Bilbo Baggins (*The Hobbit*, book), Jon Snow (A Song of Ice and Fire), Black Widow (Marvel), Jesse Pinkman (*Breaking Bad*), the Cowardly Lion (*The Wizard of Oz*, 1939), Dwight Schrute (*The Office*), Chidi Anagonye (*The Good Place*), Peter Pettigrew/Wormtail (Harry Potter), Grima Wormtongue (Lord of the Rings)

DEEP DIVE: CHIDI ANAGONYE

It's probably not a shocker that one of the favorite shows of a Type 1 satire writer like me is The Good Place. *I think about jokes from that show at least once a week, even years after it wrapped. So, when it came time to pick a Six for this deep dive, selecting Chidi felt like a little treat I could give myself as well as a solid example of how to write a Six that is incredibly likeable and incredibly flawed. While Chidi's character arc continues beautifully through all four seasons of the show, this deep dive will focus specifically on the first season. That way, if you haven't watched* The Good Place, *you only have to watch the first season if you want to see more of what I'm describing in the analysis. I'm also going to spoil the big Season One twist for you in this analysis, so if you don't want that, then watch the first season before reading. Then you can watch the other three seasons just for funsies.*

Analysis: When the show's protagonist, Eleanor Shellstrop, first discovers she's died and gone to The Good Place, she knows right away there's been a mistake. She's not the Eleanor whose memories are attached to her name. In fact, she's a big fraud, not even an *okay* person, let alone one who's good enough to make the cut for The Good Place.

Everyone in The Good Place has a soul mate ready for them, and Eleanor's is Chidi Anagonye, a Senegalese professor of ethics, and presumably a very good person.

Our first big sign that Chidi is a Six is his commitment to his word and loyalty to his perceived soul mate. Once they're alone together in their house, she asks if she can trust him not to tell anyone what she's about to say. He agrees before having a clue as to the topic, and she drops a bomb that launches him in a terrible ethical dilemma: she's not supposed to be there. There's been a mistake and she's not the Eleanor Shellstrop that the architect of the neighborhood, Michael, believes her to be. It's not his death but rather *this* development, where Chidi's vow of loyalty makes him complicit in afterlife subterfuge, that constitutes the inciting incident for his character arc.

Keeping Eleanor's secret is a non-negotiable for him, but does protecting her lie also make him a bad person undeserving of being in The Good Place?

To the Enneagram newbie, "professor of ethics" might ping on your radar for a One. Ones are the highly ethical and principled type, after all. It's not a bad starting point for a theory. But we get more clues as the show progresses that the problem isn't Chidi's innate and stringent sense of right and wrong, but rather his *disconnection* from that internal compass that leaves him constantly searching for answers from perceived authority figures like Aristotle, Plato, and Kant. Ones start from their gut when it comes to right and wrong, but Sixes come at it from the position of the head, or logic. This is a crucial difference and ends up being the crux of Chidi's issues throughout the show.

Chidi is likeable because he wants to do the right thing, and that makes a character extremely sympathetic. But he's flawed because he's stuck in anxiety and doubt about what is "right." The options presented to those in the afterlife are The Good Place or The Bad Place, a binary distinction. If you don't qualify for The Good Place, you'll be tortured for eternity in The Bad Place. Those are the rules, and rather than questioning the rules right away, Chidi accepts them and finds himself with a terrible ethical dilemma as a result: Does he opt for honesty and tell Michael that Eleanor isn't supposed to be in The Good Place (ergo: she should be tossed into the place with all the torture, which is extreme for the level of her petty misdeeds), or does he keep his promise to Eleanor to spare her that fate and in doing so risk his own goodness by hiding a lie?

If Chidi were a One, his first instinct would likely be to reject the framing of the question altogether. In true Reformer fashion, he would say, "That's a stupid system. How do we change it?" But he's not a One, he's a Six, and the Six is trying to stay safe, supported, and looks to guidance from authority to do that. Changing the system (which seems divine and eternal in nature) doesn't occur to him. Instead, he tries to make Eleanor into a good person so that his dishonesty doesn't feel so dishonest and he doesn't get in trouble.

Not getting in trouble, or at least an awareness of what would get one in trouble, is never far from the mind of the Six. Chidi is a typical phobic Six, so he's thinking about how to *avoid* getting in trouble. Notice how the idea of "getting in trouble" involves an *external* authority to get in trouble with. This is a result of Sixes losing touch with their internal authority (or inner moral compass) and seeking it externally. Even counterphobic Sixes have an awareness of what might get them in trouble; they simply deal with their anxiety by rushing full-force into the trouble. Chidi is always trying to find the loophole that will keep him out of trouble.

This detachment from inner guidance causes Sixes like Chidi all kinds of anxiety and leads them into the vice of Doubt. Chidi's extreme degree of doubt is a running joke of the show, as we learn that he once had a panic attack during a game of rock-paper-scissors. Michael frequently defers to Chidi to make decisions, which is torture for the ethics professor and one of our biggest red flags that The Good Place might not be all that it seems. At one point, while Michael is encouraging Chidi to get some hobbies, he presents Chidi with a telescope to stargaze. Chidi kindly refuses the offer, saying that he's been described as "directionally insane." Being as full of doubt as Sixes can be, "directionally insane" may feel familiar to many of them. When you don't have the sense of where you stand, how do you orient yourself?

As the storyline progresses and Chidi does his best to teach Elanor how to be a good person so she can remain hidden as a fraud, we learn more about his life back on Earth. Michael presents Chidi with the draft of the ethics book Chidi was working on, which is currently 3,600 pages and still unfinished. Michael tells him it's unreadable, in part because he's constantly contradicting himself throughout it.

This is a central problem with Chidi's strategy for soothing his core fear: if you defer to the authority of the great philosophers for your moral compass, you're screwed from the start because *they don't agree with each other.* This trap is laid for any Six who refers to authorities for answers that can only be found internally. Inevitably, the Six encounters authorities who disagree with one another, as is the case for Chidi and the reason why his manuscript is already 3,600 pages.

Chidi ties himself in knots when it comes to taking action on anything involving ethics. But when Michael finally discovers that Eleanor is an imposter and is about to send her away to The Bad Place, something breaks loose in Chidi, who has created a bond with Eleanor, cracking the armor of his overactive Head Center. He advocates for Eleanor, saying she's become a much better person since being in The Good Place and studying under him. His Heart Center is waking up and inspiring him to talk back to authority. Michael replies, "There's no award for Most Improved Player." Astoundingly, Chidi barks back, "Well, maybe there should be!"

It's a crucial moment of character development for Chidi. He's stopped accepting the authority's rules as a given. He's moved from *thinking* about righteousness to *feeling* it in his body, standing on all ten toes and speaking up, pushing back against the rules. This takes a great deal of courage, which is something he's gained from Eleanor's complete disregard of authority and general brazenness. Chidi seems to surprise even himself with this pushback.

It doesn't work, but he's just connected to something in himself that he doesn't forget, and that allows him to fight against the system to keep Eleanor and the other likeable impostor he discovers from being tortured for eternity.

Granted, he's not "cured" of his doubt by any means (we never move past our vice completely). At one point, when Chidi can only spare one of three people he knows from being taken to The Bad Place and must choose which, Michael tries to help Chidi connect with a gut instinct through offering him three frozen yogurt options, pressuring him to *just pick one!* Chidi's response is, "Let me think about that!"

Chidi's loyalty is never in question, though, and that's what keeps him sympathetic. When Eleanor tries to push him away to keep him out of trouble, he replies, "I'm in this. We're a team." This is why it's so wonderful to have a Six as a friend. And for Eleanor, who's always been on her own and was raised by the two most selfish people in Phoenix, Arizona, his loyalty is a lifeline. They may not be soul mates, but they're the balm to each other's wounds.

Chidi's pursuit of goodness is narratively load-bearing for the first season. So long as we believe that Chidi is a good person worthy of being in The Good Place, then those in The Good Place (and the audience) will continue carrying on with the assumption that what we're seeing and being told is "The Good Place" really is. We learn that Eleanor and

Jason are mistakes, and Tahani certainly seems iffy, but Chidi is a good person, so everything must be what it seems.

This presumption is what allows the twist at the end of Season One to be so gratifying. When Eleanor cracks the code and realizes that this *isn't* The Good Place after all and is, in fact, The Bad Place, we're consequently offered a verdict on Chidi's perceived righteousness. He's NOT a good person. He doesn't belong in The Good Place.

He's *contemplated* ethics his whole life, but his indecision and doubt have kept him from ever enacting it and have, in fact, caused harm (and led to his own death). "No, dingus," says Michael, spelling it out once his true nature as a demon is revealed. "You hurt everyone in your life with your rigidity and your indecisiveness."

Chidi was never pursuing goodness after all. He was always seeking avoidance of getting into trouble with an authority for "being bad." There's a difference, and the difference is, according to the show, a determinant for getting into The Good Place or The Bad Place.

Eleanor sums up how she realized that they were, in fact, in The Bad Place, when she describes it as a "filthy dumpster full of our worst anxieties." They were set up to torture *one another*. When you reflect back, this is exactly what happens to Chidi. He's put in a moral dilemma right away that he doesn't know how to navigate and that he can't ask the person in charge to help him out with. He's forced to make weighty decisions left and right, forced to be loyal to someone who behaves selfishly, and is constantly confronted with the consequences of his hesitation. There is no Badder Place for a Six. Only a storyteller could conceive of such a brutal *contrapasso* for someone whose sins are woven from anxiety and doubt.

But there are still small signs of a change within Chidi throughout the first season—when he considers the possibility of a new system, showing courage to protect the people he's grown to care about. He may be in The Bad Place, but all is not lost. He's showing growth, and that's something Michael the architect doesn't account for in his devious plans.

While Chidi's knowledge of philosophy, morality, and ethics doesn't keep him from being sent to The Bad Place, it does become the key to this small band of friends learning what each other needs for the survival of all in an openly hostile environment—an essential gift of the Six, once they can muster in themselves the courage for it.

TYPE 7

TYPE NAMES

The Enthusiast, the Joyful Perspective, the Enthusiastic Visionary, the Epicurean, the Generalist, the Energizer, the Multi-tasker

CORE MOTIVATIONS

Fear: of being trapped in pain or deprivation

Desire: to be satisfied

The Seven's core motivations present themselves in novelty and pleasure seeking.

BRIEF DESCRIPTION

Sevens are attuned to what feels good. They like to keep things fun and interesting, seeking novelty and sometimes even thrills. The like the new toy, the new idea, the new sensation, the variety of an endless scroll on their phones.

They shy away from anything painful, whether that's physical, mental, emotional, or spiritual pain. When they sense that first twinge of it, their attention shoots toward whatever pleasurable escape seems most promising. There are so many pleasurable things in the world, the Seven doesn't understand why so many people seem intent on staying in pain … and ask the Seven to sit in that pain, too.

Sevens see the world as full of future promise. The future is always a pleasurable diversion for Sevens, and we see that through the pleasure they experience from making plans. *Keeping* those plans is not as appealing, though. To a Seven, making plans is living in future possibility, but keeping the plans is limiting themselves to being in one place and time. And what if they're not in the mood to keep the plans when the time comes? Why deprive themselves of something better?

Problems arise for Sevens when they spend too much time in the future, which doesn't exist. What they're really doing is seeking a hit of pleasure in their imagination, but the fleeting pleasure the Seven gains from these diversions does not create the deep satisfaction they truly desire. Without mitigation, the Seven can end up with a life ruled by the need for one easy but short-lived hit of dopamine after another, leaving a lot of unfinished projects and broken promises in their wake. In this way, the Seven thwarts their attempt to secure the one thing they want: something to finally satisfy them.

The loop that Sevens oftentimes find themselves in, of spending too much money, drinking or partying in excess, taking big risks that don't generally pay off, and leaving friends in the lurch by flaking on plans, arises from the mistaken belief that satisfaction is something one must actively and sometimes frantically seek, rather than something one learns to access and connect with in the present moment.

Only when the Seven slows down and learns to tolerate the pain of that restless feeling that accompanies limitation can they start to tap into the unending fullness of each moment. This is a big process that most Sevens don't have any interest in trying. As the type most affected by FOMO (fear of missing out), the Sevens trick themselves into believing that satisfaction lies in all the things they're *not* doing, rather than in the only place where it can ever be found: right in their present moment. But to learn that, they must practice focusing their attention on the present rather than escaping into other times and places as their fear is triggered.

When the Seven cuts out everything from their life that might be painful, they miss out on a richness of life that's a necessary ingredient to satisfaction. The Seven likely isn't aware that they're cutting out all the painful moments, as the word they use for the pain of sitting still and confronting human limitations of time and space is usually "boring" rather than "painful." For the Seven, "this is boring" is how they say, "I'm bumping up against the pain of restlessness caused by experiencing deprivation." The idea of being fully present in any given moment may make the Seven feel as though they are missing out on everything else, and their unsatisfying solution is to try to experience as much as they can—and they often succeed, right to the point where their attention is never on what is but rather on what isn't.

Once Sevens learn the ways they've been depriving themselves of the richness of life, they may be more open to experiencing the discomfort necessary to be in the present. They may be willing to label their restlessness as fear, finally, and their pleasure seeking as an expression of anxiety. Their gluttony for new experiences may lessen as they prefer to build a more mindful life. Rather than taking the stance of "more is more," they may begin to understand how "less is more."

Instead of tasting every chocolate in the display case, they might find themselves satisfied with simply picking one and eating it with their full attention, enjoying the scent, flavors, and textures fully. Rather than having a lot of friends with whom the relationship stays fairly surface-level, they may realize they'd rather have a few friends they see more than once a month and with whom they can go deep into the scary and dark parts of life with to create a satisfying intimacy. Instead of viewing responsibility to others as yet another limitation on their freedom, they learn that responsibility to others can be path toward the deep satisfaction they've been seeking.

WINGS

7w6

The Six wing can provide a useful anchor for an energetic and novelty-seeking Seven. The Six will pull the Seven's attention more toward finding security through relationships rather than always seeking security through endless possibilities, grounding them in something solid and providing a constant in the rotating door of their lives. The Six wing will also encourage the Seven to occasionally approach new tasks and experiences with a useful amount of caution, rather than focusing on what could go right and ignoring possible complications. This allows the Seven to keep from bailing on projects and friendships where their blind spot didn't see the warning signs and they dove in too quickly. Meanwhile, the anxious patterns of the Six can lead the Seven to be quicker to startle and bail, ditching a project or relationship at the first sign of trouble rather than sticking around.

The Six wing keeps the Seven more socially focused but slightly more reserved. It also plants the thinking-avoidant Seven more firmly into the Thinking Center, possibly encouraging them to pause and consider before acting.

7w8

The Eight wing brings a boldness and vitality to the Seven that leads them to be more focused on getting what they want and can narrow the scope of their attention. It can add a degree of drive that helps them push past the initial pain points of a process or relationship to get to something more satisfying. The Eight wing can also get them into trouble, as its vice of Lust combines with the Seven's vice of Gluttony into a mentality of "I want it all and I want it now." This can lead to the Seven ignoring the complaints or needs of others in their pursuit for more now.

The Eight wing helps nudge the Seven more toward the Action Center, encouraging them not to sit in the pleasure of mentally planning but to also take action toward the satisfaction of completion. On the other hand, it can encourage the Seven to launch into action without thinking about how it might affect others or how the Seven's plate may already be full with other things that are knocked off without consideration.

LEVELS OF DEVELOPMENT

Healthy: Able to sit with and process complicated experiences, feels gratitude and appreciation, enjoys the simple wonders of the world, enthusiastic about a wide range of experiences, discerning between spontaneity and impulsiveness, ability to focus on the present allows for great achievements, vivacity leads to accomplishments in many areas.

Average: Increasing restlessness splits focus, always seeking more options, variety and pleasure take precedent over depth and richness, loses sight of priorities as hyperactivity takes over, impulsive, exaggerated storytelling or performing to be seen as fun and interesting, becomes a spring of ideas with no follow-through, overconsumes and prone to a variety of excesses, unable to feel satisfied, gluttonous.

Unhealthy: Lacks impulse control, governed by selfish pleasure seeking, loses control of pleasure-pain balance and falls into addictions, cannot face basic discomfort of daily life, flees responsibility, becomes erratic and compulsive, eventually runs out of energy and crashes out in panic and despair.

VICE

The Seven's vice is **Gluttony**. This looks like seeking satisfaction through quantity rather than quality of experience. They abuse their sense of optimism to reject the idea of limitation, which they equate to deprivation, and try to get everything they want all at once, particularly novel sensations and experiences. This pursuit leaves them just as unsatisfied as before, which tends to accelerate the intensity of their seeking.

Your Type 7 character will get themselves into trouble by trying to do too much and letting the important and fulfilling parts of life slip away. They may also act recklessly in their pursuit to enjoy life.

VIRTUE

The virtue of the Seven is **Sobriety**. Only once the Seven can reject their Gluttony that causes them to do things in excess can they experience the state of Sobriety, or moderation. As the Seven learns that what is here and real is always more satisfying than what is over there and imaginary, their frenetic quests slow, and they can exist in the here-and-now, trusting that that it offers not limitation and deprivation, but abundance to those who seek it.

STRESS TYPE

Moves toward One. As the Seven's desire to do all the things without missing out fails to produce any true satisfaction, the stress will initiate a harsh inner disciplinarian in the hopes that *they* will force the Seven to follow through on something long enough and deeply enough to gain satisfaction. In the meantime, this inner voice is cruel, punishing, and sucks all the joy from the Seven's life. If the Seven can take this stress moment as an opportunity to examine which of their many endeavors leads to the kind of life they want, they can connect with a healthy inner discipline that leads them toward joyful fulfillment through a gentle narrowing of focus.

GROWTH TYPE

As the Seven realizes that their fear of missing out is making them miss out on the only thing they will ever truly have, the present, they can access the focus and simplicity of the Five. They begin to see that satisfaction and gratitude can only be found in what they have, not in those things they do not have, and shift from a "more is more" to a "less is more" mindset.

COMMON THEME PAIRINGS

Joy, pain, fear, avoidance, reality, contentment, responsibility, abundance/scarcity, satisfaction, freedom, faith

TRIAD/CENTER

Head/Thinking/Cognitive

Sevens are often surprised to learn that they're in the Thinking Center of the Enneagram, because they tend to look more like Action or Feeling types. But their Head Center is always active, imagining future possibilities that might bring pleasure and a distraction from the low-grade anxiety they experience in their daily life.

Sevens enjoy imagining the future, particularly a positive one full of their favorite experiences and plenty of novelty. In this way, they display a sort of conceptualizing, except it's about possibilities rather than realities. To be clear here, it's not the *realization* of future possibilities that the Seven craves, but the *imagining* of it taking place in their minds. That is the escape.

The Seven tends to be a quick thinker, not wanting to get bogged down (i.e., deprived) in the step-by-step, and so they leap ahead. Deliberating over a decision is physically painful for a Seven, and they avoid it as much as possible. They don't mind jumping into something quickly, because if it's not as pleasurable as they'd anticipated, they're usually okay jumping right out of it and into something else.

The Seven's thinking often takes the form of planning. This looks like thinking through their plans for the future. The problem is that imagining plans can be much more pleasurable for the Seven than executing them, which often requires hard work and sticking with the execution through the painful parts that the planning process glossed over. In this way, the Thinking Center gets its hit of pleasure at the expense of the Action Center, which is then tasked with actually getting shit done.

Anxiety/Scarcity/Security

Because Sevens tend to be bright-siders, relying on sublimation to skip over feeling unpleasant feelings by jumping straight to the silver lining, they're not usually identified as being anxious individuals. But they are. Their anxiety takes the form of restlessness, being unable to sit in silence, and flailing if they don't have a sunny future to disappear into. Until they learn to identify these feelings as anxiety, they cannot confront the fear, and *only* through confronting the fear can they discover that being still, present, and at ease in the moment is not something to spend one's life running from.

Like every type, Sevens grow sick of the same old problems their patterns create, and by seeing that their patterns are, in fact, creating repetition rather than novelty, they may become more open to trying something new; namely, exploring the restless feeling of "boredom" rather than immediately trying to distract themselves from it.

Because Sevens are terrified of deprivation, anything that feels like scarcity will likely launch them into action. They grope around externally for satisfaction that cannot be found externally but can only be attained through internal practices of appreciating what is and feeling true gratitude for what they already have. By mistaking scarcity as an external situation rather than a pattern of thinking and feeling, they never address the true cause of their anxiety and can, over time, spiral into addictive, pleasure-seeking behaviors that run their life and lead them into severe financial, emotional, relational, and spiritual deprivation.

If the Seven practices impulse control around their anxious behaviors, rejecting the idea that the next hit of pleasure will be the one that guarantees them security, they'll begin to connect with the satisfaction of delayed gratification. In other words, only by experiencing the pain of depriving their impulses will they adequately challenge their anxiety so they can experience deep satisfaction.

INTERACTION STYLE

Sevens are an **assertive** type. They don't trust that what they need will find them, so they depend on getting the resources and security they want. They do this through a "more is more" mindset with things like shopping, experiences, and relationships. Why wait on what they want when they can chase after it right now?

DIALOGUE

Not only does the Seven avoid boredom at all costs, they don't want to inflict it on others. One of the ways this emerges through their speech is excitement and hype. When they find something that love—restaurant, TV show, vacation spot—they want to share all the fun of it with those around them. They will share the highlights and leave out the lowlights ... or spin the lowlights into an entertaining story. They'll also hype up their friends, wanting to make those around them feel good and happy. They make excellent cheerleaders for the zany ideas of those around them—the stranger and more novel the idea, the more the Seven will support it. When you tap into writing a Seven, you may feel like you're abusing the exclamation point, but if you're not a Seven, you may not be using it enough (Sevens frequently report having to scrub this punctuation mark from their emails because it turns up at the end of every sentence).

They often reply in the affirmative and emphatically so. "Absolutely!" "Fantastic!" Even if they don't agree with the other person, they may start off by agreeing and rather than arguing, simply offer their stance *also*—after all, why limit the conversation to a single viewpoint? "Oh, totally! I could also see that ..." and then they present a different viewpoint entirely.

Sevens make entertaining storytellers, and combined with some of the unusual activities they get up to, this can result in them holding court during group conversations, not because they need or demand the attention, but because they genuinely capture their audience's attention. Over time, the Seven develops a sixth sense for what is entertaining and enrapturing, and they like to share that talent with anyone who'll listen.

If the Seven isn't quite the adventuring type (some are not), their ability to spin even a shitshow into a comedy routine makes them engaging storytellers. You'll often hear them cracking jokes at the expense of their own dignity, if that's what it takes to raise the spirits of those around them. Something as simple as a dressing-room snafu the Seven had might be the story of the night that everyone is laughing to themselves about the next day.

STEREOTYPES

The Seven is often presented as the class clown, the good time, or the adventure buddy, and they often are all those things in comparison to the other types. But Sevens can also get depressed. This is sometimes a product of failing to develop tools to deal with the unpleasant emotions and situations we sometimes find ourselves in or the general horrors that exist in the world, which the Seven eventually struggles to escape. In the event that their coping mechanism of sublimation fails, and they simply cannot find a silver lining, the Seven can fall very deep into a dark hole. And in that dark hole, they find all those unpleasant emotions that they skipped over for so long. This dark hole feels like it might last forever, and can trigger the most intense fear response from them, as they feel like they've landed in hell itself, an inescapable place full of nothing but pain and deprivation. Reckless behaviors tend to follow.

They must do something, anything, to tap into pleasure and distraction again.

Sevens aren't all energy and enthusiasm all the time, though they may appear that way to others. Instead, they often live in boom-and-bust cycles, disappearing from view when they're in the low-energy state. The dark side of their enthusiasm is that while being entertaining and "fun" makes them feel good, they can also feel pressured to put on a show when around others (it's what the people want and expect!) to keep the mood light. The Seven may push themselves too hard to appear high-energy and exciting so that they collapse, exhausted, as soon as they're alone.

Not all Sevens start from scratch with zero pain tolerance. If a Seven is forced to endure an experience that didn't allow them to avoid the pain, such as an early, unavoidable loss or tragedy, they may have a higher pain tolerance or an appreciation for the deeper levels of life pain allows them to access. These Sevens reach for happiness through gratitude rather than pleasure seeking and are much more grounded as a result. Not every Seven gets spooked and flees at the first sign of pain or responsibility (though this does tend to be the case on the whole).

EASY MISTAKES TO MAKE

Because Sevens tend to be sunny and friendly, writers often blend them with the Two or the Nine. The three types all fall into the "positive outlook" or "avoidant" approach to conflict, but they use different tools for it. Focusing on the positive allows the Seven to avoid pain, so they silver-line where they can, as quickly as they can (sublimation). Looking for the positive in a situation is not in itself a problem, and neither is being able to imagine interesting options for the future, but it does become an issue for the Seven when they *skip over* the part of feeling the pain, anger, fear, or loss before latching on to the bright side. It's also not uncommon for them to herd others toward the bright side, too, which can injure relationships (it's often seen as expressing "I do not accept this version of you" to someone who is already struggling).

Positivity is not exclusive to Sevens, but they are one of the three "positive outlook" types in the way they deal with conflict (along with Twos and Nines). Sevens stay positive to avoid the pain of deprivation or feeling trapped, while Nines present a positive exterior to avoid acknowledging conflict, and Twos present a positive exterior to avoid burdening anyone with their emotions.

It may all look like "cheering up" others, but the *motivations* behind doing so hold important differences. This distinction becomes especially important when writing from that character's POV.

EXAMPLES

Peter Pan, Merry and Pippin (Lord of the Rings), Fred and George Weasley (Harry Potter), Ariel (Disney's *The Little Mermaid*), Barbie (*Barbie*, 2023), Anne Shirley (*Anne of Green Gables*), Tigger (Winnie the Pooh), Hermes (Greek mythology), Dionysus (Greek mythology), Will Smith (*The Fresh Prince of Bel Air*), Deadpool, "The Capitol" (Hunger Games)

DEEP DIVE: ANNE SHIRLEY

First published in 1908, Anne of Green Gables *has experienced a resurgence of popularity lately, so I thought it would be interesting to look into what makes this particular character iconic, even so many years later. The internet seemed pretty certain that she was a Four with her wild imagination and intensity of emotional expression. I went into my close reading expecting for that to be true. That's not what I saw emerge when I looked deeply at her motivations, though. That's why I've selected her as my Type 7 example. She shows us why it's important to differentiate between traits and motivation, because in certain cases, there may be a cluster of traits typically associated with one type, but the motivation behind them doesn't align with that assumed type.*

We're going against the rule of not typing young people, but since she's a fairly developed character, and just a character, we can break that rule for the sake of analysis.

Analysis: When we first meet Anne Shirley, she's an eleven-year-old orphan waiting to be picked up at a train station by strangers. One would normally assume some anxiety associated with her predicament, so we have our first glimpse into how she deals with uncertainty and what shape her fear may take right off the bat. Children try on all kinds of approaches to life, so you even if you have a guess on type, you want to hold it loosely. On the other hand, there are some young people where the type is so obvious that it's hard to avoid. We see that in Anne, as her approach to a stressful situation is generally to seek out things that distract her from the pain.

This is where I first went, "Huh," about her type. Fours are imaginative like Anne, yes, but what they use that imagination to achieve versus how Anne uses hers are quite different. Anne isn't worried about being unique, as Fours are. She's not using her imagination to prolong melancholy or intensify complicated emotions of the situation, which would be an easy thing to do for an abandoned orphan at a train station. Abandonment is a huge vulnerability for Fours, a sore spot that they may see in more places than it truly exists, and yet in this situation where Anne is objectively abandoned, she doesn't choose to see her life that way. The abandonment doesn't even seem to register.

Anne seeks beauty, yes, but her search for it is always externally focused, and she doesn't struggle in the least bit to find it. She sees the world through rose-colored glasses, to be sure, which is much more a hallmark of a Seven, who's avoiding pain and deprivation, than a Four, who's avoiding feeling ordinary and without significance.

The town of Avonlea is what many would call a very ordinary and boring farming town, but rather than allow herself to experience the fear of deprivation, Anne imagines for herself a wonderful, beautiful, and sparking world where everything has a name.

There are bits of her that speak to the Four, certainly. Her obsession with the "romantic" hints toward one of the descriptive names of the Four, "the Romantic." But romance for Anne, even some of the tragic romances she imagines up in her story club with Diana, are romantic in a *pleasurable* way, as a Seven would appreciate. They seem light, not heavy.

Anne is a specific instinctual subtype of the Seven—the "SX 7," called either the Sexual 7 or the One-on-One Seven. This subtype shows us why it's so important to look at *motivation*, not trait, because on the outside, these Sevens may look like a dreamy, dramatic, and even moody Four, but behind it all is a need to escape confinement and deprivation in the world around them, not a longing for something that's missing from them.

To put a sharper point on it, Anne functions significantly more out of the Seven's vice of Gluttony than the Four's vice of Envy. "I wanted to see everything that was to be seen on that boat," she tells Matthew on their ride back from the train station, "because I didn't know whether I'd ever have another opportunity."

We see a clear indicator of her motivation for always losing herself in romantic imaginations when she says, "It's all very well to read about sorrows and imagine yourself living through them heroically, but it's not so nice when you really come to have them, is it?" Her imagination is a place for her to escape to for pleasure and to avoid pain and boredom, even the tragic scenarios she conjures up. They don't hit deep but stay on the surface of play. They're a way of avoiding rather than leaning into the pain of her past.

Anne lights up a room when she walks in, even as her nonstop talking initially annoys the shit out of almost every adult she meets. She has a positivity and resilience that we see through the patterns of the Seven to keep an eye on future possibilities and put blinders on to the pain of the past. In the brief history Anne gives the woman who adopts her (Marilla), we see that there is plenty of pain to be found in her life. Anne doesn't stew on it, though: "Anne finished up with another sigh, of relief this time. Evidently, she did not like talking about her experience in a world that had not wanted her."

It may be easy to connect her abandonment with the Four's vulnerability to abandonment, but this is a great case of how themes like this can be more situational than fundamental. Not every orphan who's been abandoned is a Four. Were Anne *also* a Four, on top of being an orphan, we could expect to see this idea of "I will be abandoned" play out more significantly in her relationships, likely through creating a push-pull dynamic where she abandons others before they can abandon her. Instead, she builds solid relationships with wide-eyed enthusiasm typical of a Seven, and she fights for them.

We almost never hear of her history (from her) again, except for when she uses her previous experience with the croup to save the Berrys' child. This is standard operating procedure for a Seven, who doesn't hold on to their pain as an important part of their autobiography, as Fours tend to. In fact, Anne doesn't seem to hold on to any particular story about herself that she returns to, but rather enjoys making up one after another, holding each lightly and discarding it when it becomes dull.

We're treated to a wonderful moment of her Seven-ness when Anne stares at a depiction of Jesus on Marilla's wall. Anne hasn't been brought up with religion, so she brings a fresh perspective to something Marilla is fully committed to.

Anne says, "But I wish the artist hadn't painted Him so sorrowful looking. All His pictures are like that, if you've noticed. But I don't believe He could really have looked so sad or the children would have been afraid of Him."

Marilla chides her for being blasphemous, but Anne doesn't relent. Her biggest complaint about church, once she begins attending, continues to be the lack of joy and enthusiasm she sees there. In fact, the gift of the Seven is joy, and it's not surprising to see her annoyed that there's so much focus on all the pain. But joy also has a place in the Christian tradition ("Joy to the world," for starters), and Anne brings that to a household and community that has placed appropriateness and tradition above everything else.

Anne's hot temper may come as a surprise for those getting acquainted with this Enneagram type, but it's not a surprise to anyone who's met a Seven with a strong Eight wing. We see her temper flare when Mrs. Lynde insults her appearance upon their first meeting. Anne tells her off, defending herself with the fire and advocacy of her strong and bold Eight wing. When Marilla tells her she must apologize to Mrs. Lynde, Anne responds, "How can I? I'm *not* sorry. I'm sorry I've vexed you; but I'm *glad* I told her just what I did. It was a great satisfaction. I can't say I'm sorry when I'm not, can I? I can't even *imagine* I'm sorry."

The word "satisfaction" stands out to me here, as it's the core desire of the Seven and a clear motivator for Anne's response to Mrs. Lynde. Anne struggles to seek satisfaction at every turn, avoiding whatever pain is closing in on her in any moment.

If you're writing a Seven, you'd be hard pressed to write more on-point dialogue than some of the following from Anne:

"Oh, Marilla, looking forward to things is half the pleasure of them. You mayn't get the things themselves; but nothing can prevent you from having the fun of looking forward to them."

"But really, Marilla, one can't stay sad very long in such an interesting world, can one?"

"I never knew before that religion was such a cheerful thing. I always thought it was kind of melancholy, but Mrs. Allan's isn't, and I'd like to be a Christian if I could be one like her."

"It isn't very pleasant to be laid up; but there is a bright side to it, Marilla. You find out how many friends you have."

One of the reasons Anne stands out as such an iconic character against the backdrop of rural Canada is the influence she has on those around her. You see the gifts of her Seven-ness seep into everyone around her, especially her caretakers. Matthew (likely a Nine) is happy to absorb her influence, but Marilla (certainly a One) doesn't let Anne's joy and lightness penetrate her life without a fight.

Over the years, though, not even Marilla's rigidity can withstand the playful imagination, optimism, and hope that Anne brings everywhere she goes. The adults who interact with her become lighter. They laugh more. Even as they shape her, she shapes them. The whole town of Avonlea seems to brighten once the foreign body of Anne is introduced. The reader is treated to seeing Anne through various perspectives as they experience this spiritual brightening.

As Anne matures and learns to armor herself more from the harshness of life that has so frequently blindsided her and caused her pain, Marilla begins to sense the loss and mourns it. Anne is less talkative, more studious and serious. She has begun to wrangle herself to spare herself the pain of the lows, but in so doing loses the exuberance of the highs.

We see this trend continue as Anne attends school in the city, studying to be a teacher. The natural beauties that used to bring her delight in Avonlea are replaced by something she finds just as pleasurable: ambition. She sees it as a future promise she can look forward to and anticipate.

Her enthusiasm for winning and dreaming of the future helps her develop a focus that she didn't always have and earns her the many open doors she was hoping for. Sevens love nothing more than an abundance of promising options. But this is where her biggest test begins.

Tragedy back home and a growing need for her assistance at Green Gables creates a fork in the road: pursue her dream of going to a university or return to Avonlea and to teach and care for Marilla. Rather than feeling trapped or claustrophobic from the latter option, Anne has matured enough to realize that she can lean into her responsible Six wing to care for the person she loves most *and* the future can remain full of possibilities, even if her present may feel limiting and familiar. This is a fairly healthy expression of her type; she anchors herself in love rather than fleeing in fear. As she does this, she feels true satisfaction, and a new possibility blooms for her: romance with her longtime rival.

While Anne's Seven-ness may become more refined over time, it never fully goes away. She still lifts up those around her and is skilled at comforting those she cares about, lightening their load. She doesn't sit with her suffering but rather turns her attention to everything that *isn't* suffering in this world, of which there is plenty, even in a small town like Avonlea.

THE ACTION CENTER

TYPE 8

TYPE NAMES

The Challenger, the Active Controller, the Perspective of Strength, the Protector, the Maverick, the Leader

CORE MOTIVATIONS

Fear: of being harmed or controlled

Desire: to have autonomy, be independent

The Eight's core motivations present themselves as being strong and bold.

BRIEF DESCRIPTION

Eights are attuned to power. They understand that power is based on more than a person's official title or rank. They also know that power in the hands of others is the greatest threat to their own independence and autonomy. Many Eights respond to this perceived threat by either pursuing the power for themselves or becoming hyper-independent, like a sovereign island nation.

At some point, Eights learned the lesson that no one was coming to save them. No one was going to show up to protect them when they needed it, and so they must be able to protect themselves at a moment's notice. Many take this a step further and believe they are also responsible for protecting "their people" all on their own as well. This may include their family, friends, community, or even country. The role of protector comes naturally to them.

Eights generally fall into the role of leader, because who would they want to follow? Many Eights will dispute this initially, but when you ask them if they've ever had a boss whom they were willing to follow, they usually fail to come up with an example of someone they respected to the necessary degree. This is because when an Eight makes up their mind about something, they struggle to see, let alone respect, any alternative perspectives as valid. This understandably makes it difficult for them to follow another leader.

Preferring bold and immediate action as a way to soothe their anxiety, the Eight tends to practice *fire, ready, aim,* rushing into situations and trusting that they'll learn what to do as they do it. While this mostly works out for the Eight (because they make it work), it frequently doesn't work out for others, who are left picking up the pieces of the Eight's hasty all-or-nothing approach after the Eight has forged ahead. In fact, Eights are often the last to notice the negative consequences of their words and actions, and when they pause to reflect, the trail of wreckage behind them might be so much that they'd rather deny it's there, blame others for the mess, and continue on as usual.

Eights exercise a lust for life and believe that they can bend the world to their will if they try hard enough and are strong enough. They tend to sort the world into strong and weak and do everything possible to make sure they fall into the strong category. They believe that weakness invites exploitation and harm, and having experienced that before, they are willing to do anything to avoid experiencing it again, sometimes even becoming the perpetrators in their path toward keeping the upper hand.

While Eights tend to live close to the thin line between protector and predator, once an Eight begins to understand that they hold power that cannot be taken away, they are able to see that those soft parts of themselves, the emotions that make them vulnerable and human, are what make them strong and resilient, not weak.

When the Eight can reconnect to their own innocence and the innocence of others around them (not just that of dogs and children, but full-grown adults), they find themselves less motivated to assume a "me against the world" posture and can start to show the world that real strength and power comes from the willingness to be vulnerable rather than always armoring up for battle.

WINGS

8w7

The Seven wing can bring a lightheartedness to the intensity of the Eight. It can also soften the Eight's sharp focus, allowing for more possibilities to enter into their field of vision, which can keep the Eight from running into the same wall over and over again, never considering that they could walk around it. The Seven wing can also lead the Eight toward more of a work-hard, play-hard ethic that leads to some dark alleys if an addictive personality arises.

The Seven wing invites the action-dominant Eight into the Thinking Center, allowing the Eight to see more than one path or opportunity ahead of them, rather than getting lost in dominating the moment, whatever the cost. This wing tends to be more extroverted, as you have two assertive types involved.

8w9

The Nine wing helps temper the intensity of the Eight, allowing them to sit back comfortably in their power rather than always displaying it. It creates space for others around them and makes them more receptive to the natural unfolding of life, allowing that some things happen without the Eight needing to force them to happen. On the other hand, the Nine wing can lead the Eight to tune out to the signals of their body telling them that they need rest and care, as well as making the Eight's emotions more inaccessible to them.

The Nine wing keeps the Eight firmly planted in the Action Center but pumps the brakes on actual action. This can cause the Eight to appear more introverted and less reckless, but it can also create inner frustration and a lack of access to the introspection required to resolve the frustration through trying a new course of action.

LEVELS OF DEVELOPMENT

Healthy: Willing to confront danger for a greater purpose and lasting positive legacy, sees mercy and vulnerability as signs of strength, trusts that the universe "bends toward justice," exhibits true self-confidence and stands up for themselves without going overboard, a natural leader who focuses on empowering others.

Average: Functions with extreme self-sufficiency and independence, begins denying own emotional needs, need for power and control shifts from self (empowerment) onto environment (power over others), believes their word is law and needs to be boss, becomes forceful and scary to others, not afraid to use intimidation tactics to achieve their aims, projects adversarial relationships onto those who dare to be empowered, looks for obedience from others, and can create a self-fulfilling prophecy by forcing others to band together in opposition.

Unhealthy: Ruthless to avoid being controlled, acts like a dictator, starts functioning contrary to laws and morality, willing to resort to violence, fantasies of invincibility, exhibits megalomania with emerging sociopathic tendencies, feels justified in and hungry for destruction of others, murderous.

VICE

The Eight's vice is **Lust**. This presents as a tendency toward extremes and an all-or-nothing approach to life. When they want something, they want it now, whether that be a relationship, physical possessions, power, or conquest of any other type. They bring excessive intensity to what they do, even when less would better accomplish their aims. This vice often takes the form of a work-hard, play-hard mentality that can leave quite a wake behind it.

Your Type 8 character will get themselves into trouble by bringing too much intensity into situations without pausing to think about how much is needed. Their lust for power and conquest without considering the social consequences will burn bridges and earn them enemies.

VIRTUE

The virtue of the Eight is **Innocence**. Only once the Eight recognizes how their lustful intensity is contributing to their view of the world as a hostile place can they start to experience a state of Innocence. As they learn to tolerate their own vulnerability, rather than fighting against it, they begin to recognize it in others and can access generous assumptions and compassion, which allows them to rest, remove their armor, and experience how the world can be gentle with them, if they stop preemptively poking it with a stick.

STRESS TYPE

Moves toward Five. When the Eight's attempts to force their way to their objectives are thwarted for long enough, the Eight will retreat from action and move toward the isolation of the Five. This stress response may look like strategizing and can take the form of brooding and plotting revenge on those people and things that didn't bend to the Eight's will. Not as familiar with thinking as they are with action, the Eight's thoughts can become quite circular under stress without producing a clear conclusion that leads back into action. This is especially true if the Eight is expecting to concoct a plan that will *ensure* they win the battle without sustaining any hard hits on their more vulnerable spots.

However, if the Eight can use this time to reflect on their usual approach and how it might be the root of their problems (rather than everything *else* being the problem), then they can move toward a thoughtful and responsive form of action that is more likely to bring them the results they want without resorting to force.

GROWTH TYPE

As the Eight stops fearing vulnerability and having to perform strength and independence, they can access the interdependence and kindness of their growth type, the Two. Their definition of who deserves compassion expands, eventually growing large enough to include themselves.

COMMON THEME PAIRINGS

Bravery, vulnerability, control, power, responsibility, destiny, conflict, significance, kindness, innocence, strength, leadership

TRIAD/CENTER

Body/Gut/Action

The Eight is the most demonstratively action-centered of this triad, in that they focus their action outward on the world. They act on impulse that is sometimes led by the gut, but also sometimes led by fear. The Eight's connection to their Body Center is frequently visible, since their desire to appear strong and inner intensity often leads them to intense physical activity that will build literal physical strength.

This Action Center is often overexpressed by the Eight, with them opting to take action when they might be better served by pausing to think or leaving space to feel emotions—their own and those of the people affected by their decisions. What usually happens is: the louder the emotions knock on the door, the more action and intensity the Eight will likely deploy to deny those emotions entry.

Once the Eight learns the value of thinking before acting and feeling their emotions rather than actively avoiding them, the Eight is able to take action that is truly magnanimous. They can begin to differentiate between the sensations in their gut, which allows them to stop confusing fear avoidance with their wise and instinctive intuition.

Anger/Control/Autonomy

Eights approach the world in an aggressive posture without necessarily realizing it. They take the approach of "a good offense is a good defense" and may subconsciously be putting everyone on their back foot as a way of feeling in control of a situation.

Eights don't generally think of themselves as angry people, because they usually act so quickly that the anger doesn't have time to build. However, if they've developed the belief that certain emotions make them weak (sadness, loneliness, powerlessness, abandonment, and guilt tend to be the most common they avoid), they will express almost every one of those emotions as anger and outward aggression.

When Eights feel powerless or disrespected, especially, they will bring down the hammer swiftly, sensing their autonomy is threatened. But if the Eight can learn to sit with the feeling of powerlessness and attend to the younger version of themselves who literally lacked the power to protect themselves, then the Eight can stop burning so much fuel trying to control external factors like the setting and other people. Instead, they can keep that energy as fuel for the kindness and connection that they crave but can only be found through vulnerability.

INTERACTION STYLE

Eights are an **assertive** type. They demand their autonomy and independence by exerting their will on the world around them. They believe that a strong offense is a strong defense and demand what they want before the demands of the world can possibly influence them.

DIALOGUE

Eights tend to issue orders. They may not even realize they're doing it, but others do, and many types naturally obey, assuming that anyone who speaks with such confidence knows what they're doing. Eights don't question their own authority, and as a result, they speak authoritatively with a focus on action. "This must be done."

If you find yourself writing an Eight who spends time justifying to others their thought process behind each command, you're probably not writing an Eight. If you're writing a character who starts off with small talk, you're probably not writing an Eight. If you're writing a character who openly talks about their feelings, unprompted, outside of perhaps saying, "I'm pissed off," you're probably not writing an Eight. It's not that Eights don't have thoughts and feelings; they simply don't want to waste time expressing those things when there is action to be done, and there is always action to be done.

When writing an Eight's dialogue, keep their sentences short and to the point. If you have them asking a lot of questions outside of, say, a brief, an interrogation, a deposition, or a courtroom situation where they are the lead attorney, you're diminishing their power. One trick I do when writing an Eight is to go back through their dialogue, scanning for question marks at the end of the sentence then replacing them with periods. Even when Eights ask questions, they tend to be phrased as statements: "You were entering the 7-Eleven at ten fifty-eight p.m." Not "Were you entering the 7-Eleven at ten fifty-eight p.m.?" They offer a statement, and it's up to others to confirm or deny.

It's also difficult to write a convincing Eight if you don't let them curse. Even Eights of strict faith can't seem to keep the language of aggression out of their mouths. If an Eight isn't allowed to curse to blow off steam, bad things might follow. Eights, therefore, are generally quite fluent in cursing, and often make up their own signature phrases (one of my Eight characters liked calling people a "shriveled taint," for instance). Creating a signature phrase like this for your Eight is a quick way to make them iconic in the minds of the readers. Even the more conservative readers will intuitively understand that this character can't be stopped from saying what they want to say, and that can become a delicious source of vicarious naughtiness, even for the pearl clutchers.

STEREOTYPES

Eights are often imagined as bulldozers, steamrollers, or wrecking balls—take your pick. And this is a common way that those around the Eights experience them. The Eight can get so focused on achieving their objective, come hell or high water (and they expect both), that they can leave a trail of stunned people behind them. However, it's easy to imagine that the Eight doesn't have big heart, simply because they frequently don't slow down long enough to consider the feelings of others (or their own). That couldn't be further from the truth, though. Eights love "their people" *passionately*, and they express that most easily through showing protection and care. Eights make great friends for this reason. They will be right next to you, or more likely standing in front of you, when it comes time for a confrontation with a bully. Their protection often extends to financial support; part of the reason they like to be financially independent is so they can make sure they have what they need to care for the people they consider "under their protection."

Eights are often seen in one of two roles in fiction: the borderline psychopathic villain or the lone-wolf hero. Neither one is inaccurate for the Eight's common patterns. When the Eight develops a disgust for weakness in themselves, they may project it onto others around them and then seek to destroy it. They may pull a classic victim-perpetrator switch and present those with less power than them as having more and abusing it, justifying the Eight's desire to destroy those who remind them of their *own* weakness. This certainly makes an interesting villain or antihero, but it's an extremely unhealthy version of the

Eight, and as with any type, there is so much more to them.

While it's much more common for us to experience or read about an Eight with a strong Seven wing, combining the lust of the Eight with the gluttony of the Seven to create an energy of *I want it all and I want it now*, an Eight with a strong Nine wing can be an interesting character to explore, as they tend to keep their cards closer to the vest while maintaining the typical air of confidence that we expect from the Eight. While 8w9 is one of the least common expressions of the types, it can be spellbinding to watch, as the power that emanates from this character is more reserved and creates an understated threat to anyone who tries any funny business.

EASY MISTAKES TO MAKE

It's easy to ignore the inner world of the Eight just because they keep it to themselves for the most part, but as an author, it's crucial that you let it slip out from time to time so that the Eight doesn't end up as two-dimensional. Whether Eights like it or not, their armor *does* eventually slip, and beneath it may be sadness, loneliness, insecurity, or guilt.

Make no mistake, there is more than meets the eye with Eights, so don't let their shows of strength and power distract you—that's what they're intended to do. Eights have a hard, sometimes spiky, exterior, but they're soft in the middle, and allowing readers to see that here and there is the best way to keep the Eight sympathetic throughout whatever harsh decisions they might make or any damage their intense approach might cause. Even your villainous

Eights will be more intriguing if you allow the armor to slip briefly. This might take the form of a backstory in which they were, in fact, victimized, or it could be a painful loss they're carrying with them. Even vengeance can be a sympathetic endeavor, because it means the Eight had something precious taken from them.

Though it might seem otherwise, Eights don't have an endless supply of energy. As strong as they are, and as much as they're willing to push themselves past empty, they will eventually exhaust themselves physically, emotionally, mentally, and spiritually. They will not, however, let anyone see them in this state, if they can help it, because that would require showing vulnerability (this is when they may retreat toward their stress type of Five and isolate themselves away from the view of others). It's easy to mistake them for a machine that automatically generates enough energy to never slow down. They are still human (unless they're literally a robot character) and will hit their limit, sometimes in a crash-and-burn kind of way rather than slowly rolling to a stop. In this temporary lull is where you, the author, have the opportunity to force them to confront how they've been behaving. They don't have the energy to outrun the consequences of their actions. They can learn their lessons and grow, or they can fail to learn the lessons and spiral even further.

EXAMPLES

Xena (*Xena: Warrior Princess*), Ares (Greek mythology), Dean Winchester (*Supernatural*), Wednesday Addams (*Wednesday*, 2022), Leia Organa (Star Wars), Sister Night (*Watchmen*, 2019), Arya Stark (A Song of Ice and Fire), Tyler Durden (not the Narrator, *Fight Club*), Tony Soprano (*The Sopranos*), Darth Vader (Star Wars)

DEEP DIVE: WEDNESDAY ADDAMS

Wednesday Addams, specifically the version from Netflix's TV show Wednesday, *was originally going to be my Four. Then I saw that the internet mostly thought she was a Five. Then I watched the show for myself and was like, "Boy, is she an Eight! The internet is SO bad at typing." Not only is Wednesday an Eight, but she's a sympathetic one, sadistic tendencies aside.*

I'd already completed my deep dive for an iconic Eight, but once I finished the first season of Wednesday, *I was hooked. (It also helps that, at one point, Wednesday watches* Legally Blonde *as if it's a horror film, so there's a fun tie-in.) Besides, this show was a hit in recent years, so there is likely to be more familiarity with it than there would be with my original choice for this deep dive, the iconic Daniel Plainview from* There Will Be Blood.

In the show, Wednesday is only sixteen years old, an age where we usually refrain from typing to allow for the trying on of various identities. Wednesday seems to have a strong understanding of who she is for her age, and there's a sense of un-reality about the whole show that grants us more wiggle room here. That's why I've chosen her as our iconic Eight: she's well known, interesting, and her cultural lineage has matured her character (from a development perspective) and added depth to her arc.

Analysis: One of the first things we hear from Wednesday's mouth is that she considers emotions to be weakness. Okay, then. That narrows down our type options immediately. Specifically, when I hear someone say those words, my mind jumps toward the Eight, who tends to think in terms of strong/weak and who rejects vulnerability in themselves and others.

The inciting incident of this series is telling, too. Wednesday finds her little brother Pugsley stuffed in a locker at their public school. She forces him to tell her who did this to him, and when she finds out it's boys on the water polo team, she visits them during their practice and empties two large bags of piranhas into the pool to attack them, delivering the iconic line, "The only one who gets to torture my brother is me."

While this might strike a chord with oldest siblings of any Enneagram type, in the case of Wednesday, it's clear that she considers Pugsley one of "her people," in the sense that Eights will take people into their protection … so long as they, the Eight, remain in a position of power. The line between protection and control is a thin one.

Wednesday displays a misanthropy in her interactions that is usually only observed in Fives and Eights, though it's quickly clear that what she wants above all else is autonomy like an Eight, rather than security like a Five. When she's expelled from public school for attempted murder and sent to Nevermore Academy, a school for outcasts and the alma mater of her parents, her mother Morticia makes it clear that she hopes Wednesday will follow in her footsteps (Morticia was incredibly popular). Wednesday has a visceral reaction to this, seeing it as a smothering encroachment on her independence, and she pushes back against her mother every chance she gets.

With rumors swirling that Wednesday killed a kid at her last school, she's viewed by some of her new classmates as an easy target for bullying. She senses this and does what any Eight could be expected to do to avoid that vulnerable position and claim a certain degree of power: she challenges the "queen bee" to a fencing bout. It's a close one, but ultimately Wednesday is bested, which launches a personal revenge quest against the rival that she nurses through most of the story. (There is no lower-hanging fruit to fuel an Eight's vice of Lust than a desire for revenge.) Wednesday even goes so far as to later say, "I don't believe in heaven or hell, but I do believe in revenge."

This is a great example of why readers and audiences love Eights: they say things that most of us would never allow ourselves to say but might think from time to time. We get to be "bad" vicariously through them and laugh at their complete disregard for what makes others comfortable. There's a catharsis in getting to know a character who is unapologetic, blunt, and doesn't include what people think of them on their top fifty list of concerns.

Wednesday's Seven wing makes an appearance when she sets her mind to escaping Nevermore Academy. She makes plans to do so at an off-campus festival, but when she experiences a vision of one of her classmates being brutally attacked in the nearby woods, she does what Eights do and runs toward the danger. In doing so, she nearly gets herself killed and is narrowly saved.

Her reaction?

"I would've rather saved myself." The strong independence of the Eight strikes again.

And when she's chided for charging toward danger alone, she replies, "I like being an island. A well-fortified one surrounded by sharks." This line made me laugh, as almost every Eight I've ever coached either describes themselves as an island or relates strongly to the image when I mention it. The circling sharks are a nice flourish.

As with any well-crafted narrative, the protagonist of this one drives the conflict and plot with her core motivation. As Wednesday gathers allies to her side, she's pulling in people she determines are worth her protection, like her beekeeper friend and her roommate. In fact, she tends to define friendship by who is worthy of being under her protection, and she defines "worthy," it seems, as synonymous with "harmless" or "innocent."

In taking on these responsibilities, though, she's unintentionally widening her net of what affects her at the school, because it now includes what affects "her people." That impulse, plus her total lack of acceptance of any external authority, motivates her to take an interest in what's attacking people in the woods.

The fun and games end at the midpoint of the season, during Parents' Day, when Wednesday's own parents show up and her father is accused of having evaded murder charges decades earlier. Like most Eights, she doesn't see her parents as protective figures but rather as people to protect. In that way, she's compelled to get to the truth of the matter and subsequently exonerate her father for the homicide that took place at the academy back when he was a student.

This process forces her to team up with her mother, someone she'd rather keep at arm's length to protect her autonomy. When Morticia tells Wednesday that the two of them aren't competing with one another but are allies,

Wednesday replies, "Everything is a competition, Mother." (Eights get a good chuckle out of that line, I'm sure.)

However, Wednesday allows her mother in to some extent, and in allowing in that softness, allowing herself to be influenced rather than always needing to be the one influencing, she moves up slightly in her levels of development, allowing herself to be shaped by those around her in important ways.

She is also then able to hear her mother's warning that Goody Addams, her ancestor who was targeted in that town during the witch trials and who has reached out to Wednesday through visions, should not serve her as a strong mentor so much as a cautionary tale—Goody allowed her thirst for vengeance to be her undoing. Morticia worries Wednesday might do the same (and with good reason).

Once Wednesday feels sure her autonomy is being respected, her alliance with her mother offers her one more thing that she needs to solve the mystery of what's lurking outside the gates of Nevermore: Morticia's yearbook. Before, we might safely assume Wednesday would chuck the thing in the trash without cracking it open; now, having resolved her struggle for autonomy, she no longer feels the impulse to aggressively push back against her mother's legacy at the academy. Because of this, she's able to feel a sense of curiosity about her parents' lives back when they were students like her. She cracks open the yearbook, and that's where she finds the key to unraveling the mystery.

We see more of her ambivalence to relationships thin as her rift with her roommate, who is the opposite of her and whom she finds annoyingly cheerful, affects her deeply, though she wouldn't show it to anyone.

But while Wednesday claims, "I don't bury hatchets, I sharpen them," she does eventually bury the hatchet with the "queen bee" who bested her in fencing on her first day, and only through letting go of her need for revenge on those who might not actually deserve her ire does she create the network and support necessary to take on the big-bad monster threatening the place she now calls home and the people she now (begrudgingly) considers friends. Only through loosening her grip on her armor and embracing the vulnerability required to stop sacrificing everything at the altar of strength, power, autonomy, and independence can she truly have the strength at her disposal to end the threat.

There's no more concise way to show her growth in this respect in the last episode of the season than through the big hug she gives her annoying and sunny roommate (best friend?) once the big danger is past. Wednesday will never *not* be a little murderous with psychopathic tendencies, but she learns how she can retain that part of herself while also connecting to those around her in meaningful ways.

TYPE 9

TYPE NAMES

The Peacemaker, the Adaptive Peacemaker, the Perspective of Peace, the Mediator, the Healer, the Utopian, the Optimist

CORE MOTIVATIONS

Fear: of being disconnected, cut off

Desire: to be whole and unified

The Nine's core motivations take the form of focusing on common ground rather than conflict.

BRIEF DESCRIPTION

Nines are attuned to conflict. They can sense it long before the other types and learn ways to neutralize it before it threatens connection. They approach life with gentleness and tact, hoping first and foremost not to cause a stir. This makes them generally well liked and affable people. It also makes them shrink and even disappear.

Nines make choices based on what will be uncontroversial and generally well accepted. Problems arise when the Nine forgets that everyone has an opinion and some people are just haters. Trying to stay out of the way and not cause trouble means that the Nine's ability to claim and assert their needs and desires becomes incredibly restricted. Without meaning to, the Nine will become a go-along-to-get-along person, forgetting over time what it is that they want and need.

The belief that keeps the Nine imprisoned is that conflict severs connection. Because the Nines want to stay connected to others and not be abandoned and alone, they will do just about anything to avoid engaging in conflict, but that doesn't mean that conflict doesn't exist.

Nines would rather say, "It's fine, no big deal," when being disrespected or otherwise mistreated than outwardly assert their autonomy by engaging in conflict. The problem is, conflict is a natural occurrence when two people come together. It's the product of two individual wills that are not exact duplicates coexisting. Until the Nine learns to accept that, they will keep trying to mirror the will of the other person, shoving the part of themselves that could cause conflict down, down, down. Over time, the Nine stops knowing what it is that *they* want.

The conflict avoidance of the Nine doesn't only exist in their relationships with others. They avoid *internal* conflict as well by suppressing feelings, like anger, that lead one to assert autonomy and strong boundaries. Instead, the Nine would rather tell themselves that something isn't a big deal (when it is) so they can disconnect with their anger.

When one would expect a person to reasonably feel and express anger, we instead see the Nine tamp down those feelings (called *narcotization*) with food, alcohol, video games, binge-watching TV, or anything else that numbs. The result is that the Nine finds themselves physically exhausted, struggling to get going on anything. They've burned off their action energy by suppressing the emotions that they believe will cause conflict. The irony of this is that by slipping into the numbness, they've brought upon themselves the very disconnection (from self and others) they were trying to avoid.

When the Nine stops viewing conflict as a threat to connection and instead sees that it can be a bridge to deeper connection, they are able to stop disappearing at the first sign of it and start moving toward it, using their special ability to see how people are more alike than different to reach a satisfying result for everyone involved. They become expert mediators and negotiators, and rediscover their vitality through this process.

WINGS

9w8

The Eight wing helps the Nine resist merging with others by offering a stronger sense of individuality. This supports the Nine in sensing what they want and need rather than taking on those qualities from the people around them. It also helps the Nine speak up more assertively, as they understand the value of their perspective. Frequently, though, the Eight wing is an awkward and uncomfortable appendage for the Nine, and it shows up in an explosion of anger after the Nine has held in too much anger to keep the peace and can no longer stay asleep to it. This can lead the Nine to fear anger even more, only having experienced it in scorched-earth displays that don't always yield the best consequences.

The Eight wing helps the Nine connect to their power through exercising external influence on the world around them and may help them be more outspoken as a result of being in touch with their own opinion. But it may lead the Nine to act more rashly than they mean to, creating conflict that the Nine doesn't want to deal with and tunes out rather than addressing.

9w1

The One wing helps the Nine connect to a sense of purpose that ignites action when the moment is right. This wing adds structure and organization to the Nine's sometimes diffused attention, helping them to sense what's most relevant rather than getting bogged down in all the context and possible perspectives. Meanwhile, it can also add a sense of perfectionism that keeps the Nine locked in a holding pattern, expecting there to be some "perfect" way to take action or state their needs and desires that causes no conflict or friction with others. They could be waiting forever, if they're not careful.

The One wing helps the Nine sense what right action is, meaning they tend to be more reserved until the "right" moment arises. If they can tune into their gut and not let the One's perfectionism stymie them, this can allow their actions and decisions to pack a purposeful punch. But often, to avoid external conflict, the action energy is aimed inward, trying to better themselves to a point where it feels safe to speak their mind in a way everyone must agree with.

LEVELS OF DEVELOPMENT

Healthy: Senses true wholeness and at one with self, compelled to action by desire to spread love and connection, present and alive, feels and shares a deep sense of serenity, caring and diplomatic, mediates conflicts without diminishing POVs or the importance of the conflict, exemplifies strong and compassionate communication, easily spots and communicates common ground without ignoring the differences.

Average: Views conflict as something to be avoided, begins to self-erase to accommodate others, says yes when they mean no, becomes complacent and ignores problems, starts tuning out from reality, acts emotionally neglectful to themselves and others, takes a fatalistic approach of "none of this matters anyway," frustrating in their procrastination, getting a reaction or opinion from them is like getting blood from a stone.

Unhealthy: Disassociation intensifies, disconnection turns to harmful neglect, numbs self in attempt to silence inner voice, eventually becomes catatonic as they completely self-abandon and merge with others.

VICE

The Nine's vice is **Self-Forgetting**. This takes the form of numbness to their own needs to avoid the conflict they may lead to. This neglect isn't limited to their own needs but to any reality that, if acknowledged, would compel them into action that may rock the boat. This vice also shows up as a dulling of priorities so that everything feels equally important and the Nine can ignore what they'd like and only attend to what causes little conflict, both externally and in their internal world.

Your Type 9 character will get into trouble by neglecting what is important and crucial and by pretending that nothing is the matter. Bolder and more demanding personalities will pull them into serious conflict they could've avoided by being more present and learning to say no sooner.

VIRTUE

The virtue of the Nine is **Right Action**. Only once the Nine can stop falling asleep to parts of themselves to keep the peace can they experience the state of Right Action. As the Nine awakens to their unbreakable connection with the world around them—one that can only be broken through their Self-Forgetting—they stop falling asleep to conflict and instead engage with it in effective ways that nudge the world inside them and around them toward more true harmony.

STRESS TYPE

Moves toward Six. When the Nine's tendency to ignore or tune out problems snowballs over time, they may suddenly open their eyes and see a mountain of neglected tasks, conflicts, and problems to be resolved. Moving toward the anxiety and hypervigilance of the Six, they feel the need to tackle everything at once, and in doing so can't figure out where to start. They begin catastrophizing like a Six, but this is yet another delaying tactic that keeps the Nine from taking meaningful action—they're approaching the issues from the Thinking Center rather than the Action Center. If they can muster forward momentum, they may lunge at multiple problems all at once and without much of a plan, not making productive progress and possibly creating even bigger messes for themselves.

If the Nine can use this experience to reconnect to the action energy they've been suppressing, channeling it toward one effective solution at a time, and learn that addressing issues as they arise isn't as painful in the long term as ignoring them, the Nine can bring some of that ability to address conflict into their everyday life, stop tuning out what troubles them, and work toward establishing the deeper connection they crave.

GROWTH TYPE

As the Nine learns not to fall asleep to their own needs and desires, they access the ambition, goals, and sense of self-worth of their growth type, the Three. They acknowledge that they want to be seen, and they find paths that are an effective use of their effort and energy to chase after what they want.

COMMON THEME PAIRINGS

Serenity, conflict, action, agency, loneliness, connection, avoidance, courage, responsibility, harmony, belonging, identity, significance

TRIAD/CENTER

Body/Gut/Action

The Nine can struggle to understand how they fall into this triad, as they tend to lose touch with their body and find getting started on decisive action difficult. The Nine is absolutely an intuitive type, but the action piece becomes tricky when the Nine wants to make sure that the action will cause zero conflict.

Action causes conflict. When any object moves, it meets friction. Yet the Nine still holds out hope that there may be some perfect way forward that allows for them to get what they want with zero friction with others or within themselves. If they wait for that opportunity to arise, they'll be waiting forever, or at least until they wake up to the truth that the waiting in itself causes friction with others.

The numbing process that the Nine can fall into includes their connection to physical sensations. They learn to tune out those sensations, because much of the time the sensations are a physical manifestation of emotions that the Nine doesn't wish to acknowledge. These emotions don't go away, though, and often manifest as issues with sleep— insomnia, sleep disruptions, hypnopompic and hypnogogic hallucinations, and daytime drowsiness.

It can take years of ignoring these physical sensations before the Nine's anxiety about everything they've neglected breaks through the barrier and launches them into action. Unfortunately, the action tends to be frantic and unfocused and causes conflicts the Nine hasn't necessarily developed the skills to navigate.

If they can recognize how much conflict their repressed action is causing, however, they might be more willing to choose a proactive approach to creating connection through addressing conflict.

Anger/Control/Autonomy

Nines also don't generally identify with the idea of being in this triad because "I'm not angry" and because they tend to go along to get along rather than asserting their autonomous desires by pushing back against others. But the way the Nine preserves their autonomy is through *withdrawing* the parts of themselves that they believe to be controversial. Imagine them putting those parts into a cryogenic sleep so that those parts cannot be controlled or influenced by others but are *also* not causing conflict.

Nines do have strong opinions, but they keep them out of reach of others as a way of protecting those opinions from challenges. This maneuver means that people often leave a conversation with a Nine feeling like there was a consensus when that couldn't be further from the truth. This withdrawing of their individual desires, opinions, and needs from the reach of others is how the Nine protects their autonomy. It's also how they stay in control of the situation, because make no mistake, this is a power move.

Most Nines don't identify with being angry. They say they're not angry at all, when in fact they've been suppressing it for most of their lives. In general, this anger leaks out in the form of passive aggression, and when others call them on it, the Nine might genuinely believe that's not what's happening because they've become so blind to it. Or they'll recognize that they're being passive-aggressive, but they'll maintain control of the situation through denying it —people cannot argue with denial.

Even with small bits of anger leaking through, over time the Nine will compress the anger deep inside them until, eventually, like a collapsing star, it explodes. To be clear, this is rarely a productive expression, because the target of the anger tends not to be the cause of it. This explosion creates unwanted conflict in the life of the Nine, which only reinforces their belief that anger causes disconnection.

They may not realize that if they'd learned to express the anger in smaller bits along the way, it may have led to stronger connection rather than severed connection. This explosion of anger built up over time can be an awakening for the Nine, if they let it—that they are, in fact, occasionally angry. And why wouldn't they be when they've been going along, doing what *everyone else wants to do*, for most of their lives?

Learning to spot their anger earlier and using it as energy to assert their autonomy out loud by respecting their wants and needs is how the Nine moves from numbing into right action. It shifts their approach from silencing conflict to building bridges.

INTERACTION STYLE

Nines are a **withdrawn** type. They protect their autonomy by withdrawing themselves away from the world so as not to be affected or influenced. They protect their autonomy by hiding it somewhere no one—sometimes not even they— can reach it. They don't trust that others will respect their autonomy otherwise without conflict.

DIALOGUE

Nines develop the ability to see thing from others' perspectives and to understand the opinions of others. This presents itself in speech as talking *around* a point. When asked for their input, the Nine will often present the situation from many angles without identifying their personal perspective: "I can see why someone would think/feel/do X … and I can also see why someone would think/feel/do Y …" In this way, the Nine keeps clean of possible conflict by not stating what *they* think/feel/do.

The attentional flow of the Nine toward how everything is connected and the greater context of a situation means that when they finally start talking, the story may take a while. Other types may become impatient to "get to the good part," but the Nine doesn't believe they can accurately communicate the information without the context. The Nine struggles to separate the "exciting bits" from the greater tapestry, causing the retelling to meander before rushing though any real conflict. The stories might therefore be interrupted by others or end on a flat note of which only the Nine sees the relevancy.

While it's difficult to communicate through writing, the *pacing* of a Nine's speech tends to be unhurried, with long pauses. Speaking up often requires the Nine to access a part of themselves that they tucked away for safekeeping before forgetting where they stashed it. Others might interpret these pauses as an indication that the Nine has concluded what they want to say or has simply become distracted and so will jump in with replies, which the Nine usually perceives as interruption, even though there's been a long pause. The Nine will often swallow their anger and withdraw, finding further reinforcement of the belief that what they had to say wasn't important anyway. The result of this process might manifest in lines of dialogue like, "never mind," or "it's not important anyway."

Lastly, the Nine wants to form agreement with those around them, so it's not uncommon for them to pepper conversation with, "Totally," or "that makes complete sense," and start sentences with, "Yeah," before presenting a slightly different view.

STEREOTYPES

The Nine is often depicted as lazy or unmotivated because they can fall into periods of lethargy or numbing. It's important to remember that they may be unmotivated by the same things as other types, but they definitely have motivation; it's simply to remain whole and connected, which usually looks like avoiding conflict. Therefore, the way to motivate a character who is a Nine is simple but not always easy: make conflict unavoidable.

This means you really have to put a squeeze on these characters to get them to engage in what makes a story tick: conflict. Often, that means you have to blow up their home planet, figuratively or literally, depending on the genre. You have to make numbing out and avoiding conflict the most likely thing to lead to conflict so that you close down that path of escape and force them toward the conflict you want them to engage with. Nines aren't lazy, they just need to be moved (i.e., motivated) in a specific way.

Not all Nines do everything in their power to avoid all conflict at all costs. They can learn to enjoy situations where conflict naturally and unavoidably exists (as long as it isn't centered on them) because it allows them to do what they do best: find common ground. This is how Nines end up as counselors, negotiators, and even politicians (former U.S. President Barack Obama is a Nine).

The Nine's ability to see our commonalities can become the counterweight that allows them to enjoy situations with conflict, understanding that we're more alike than different, so there's always a path forward together. These more developed Nines can be the glue that holds your band of misfit characters together.

EASY MISTAKES TO MAKE

Authors who are Nines tend to write protagonists who are Nines and then wonder why they're struggling to get the story going. The problem can almost always be traced back to conflict aversion. Stories need conflict—both internal (emotional and philosophical) and external (physical). Authors who are Nines will naturally resist this or opt only for external conflicts, neglecting the internal or interpersonal ones that generate rich energy for the narrative.

This makes it difficult to keep the story moving without throwing in random external circumstances and conflicts, to which the characters generally get along well to solve, depriving the story of the internal conflict that really keeps people turning pages. While there are genres where this low-conflict approach works to an extent (think anything "cozy"), it often leaves the narrative feeling flat and too easily resolved.

Regardless of the author's own Enneagram type, writing Nines requires creating a pressure cooker to keep them moving and claiming their own agency rather than ignoring the main conflict. You really must put the squeeze on the Nine for them to not only acknowledge that conflict exists but also that conflict-based action is *inevitable*.

Because of the Nine's tendency to withdraw into themselves, it's also easy to blend them with a Four or Five, who similarly withdraw but for different reasons. The Five withdraws their thoughts and knowledge to avoid looking foolish, the Four withdraws their self-expression to avoid abandonment, and the Nine withdraws their opinions to avoid conflict.

EXAMPLES

Frodo Baggins (Lord of the Rings), T'Challa/Black Panther (*Black Panther*, 2018) The Dude (*The Big Lebowski*), Aurora (Disney's *Sleeping Beauty*), Rue (The Hunger Games), Deanna Troi (Star Trek), Winnie the Pooh (books & movies), Dorothy Gale (*The Wizard of Oz*, 1939), Albus Dumbledore & Harry Potter (Harry Potter), Bruce Banner/The Hulk (Marvel Cinematic Universe), The Narrator (not "Tyler Durden," *Fight Club*), Lester Burnham (*American Beauty*)

DEEP DIVE: THE DUDE

There are quite a few Nine protagonists to choose from who display the hallmarks of this type excellently, but I decided to go with the Nine that most of the Nines in my life (especially the male ones) agree is an absolute icon, and that's The Dude from the movie The Big

Lebowski. *It's a wildly quotable movie with a parade of insane characters with mostly violent tendencies, and amidst all the chaos stands The Dude, wishing everyone would just chill out.*

Prior to the close viewing I did for this analysis, I hadn't watched this movie in probably twenty years, and it's even more of a doozy than I remembered. But one detail about The Dude was so perfect for the type that I really saw no choice but to use him as my deep dive: that damn rug that tied the whole room together.

Analysis: The voiceover intro of this film sets the tone as it introduces the protagonist. It describes him as "the man for his time and place," and says he "fits right in." While Nines may not feel like this themselves, they are incredibly responsive to their environment and allow themselves to be influenced by it and adapt to it as a way of avoiding causing a stir. Already, we get the feeling that The Dude might be a Nine. Add in the tumbleweed metaphors—a plant that gets blown one way or another without much say in the whole thing—and, yeah, we probably have ourselves a Nine here.

After the intro, we see The Dude coming back to his apartment and getting the snot beaten out of him by two unfamiliar goons. One gives him a swirly in the toilet while the other pees on his rug. What starts out as one of the many weird details of this film—the soiled rug— becomes the catalyst for The Dude's actions and all the chaos that ensues from them.

The goons are here for a shakedown, but as it turns out, they have the wrong Jeffrey Lebowski. Yes, that's his legal name, but he's *The Dude*. He's nobody special (the Nine is given the nickname "nobody special" by Riso and Hudson in their book *The Wisdom of the Enneagram*). The goons finally leave, and The Dude is left with a piss-soaked rug that he has to throw out.

It's important to note what The Dude wears in his day-to-day life. He doesn't hesitate to be seen in public in drab and wrinkled shorts and a t-shirt covered by a worn, brown bathrobe. It's a getup so comfortable, uninspiring, and grungy that it earns comments on that account from those around him. Not all Nines dress like this, but it shows a sort of self-neglect, possibly even the vice of Self-Forgetting that we see in the Nine. It also demonstrates a preference for comfort above all else.

When The Dude joins his bowling buddies at the alley after the shakedown in his apartment, he's upset about the ordeal but doesn't necessarily show signs of doing anything about it. His anger is focused mostly on the fact that he's lost his rug that "really tied the room together." The fact that the rug really tied the room together is an apt metaphor that becomes the engine of this story. Nines are seeking unity and wholeness, in themselves, with others, and in their home environment. By ruining the rug, the goon has destroyed the peace and harmony of The Dude's home, essentially doing the very thing one must *always* do to catalyze a Nine protagonist, which is blow up their home planet.

Anger over the violation isn't yet inspiring The Dude to take any action, though. Instead, he turns his anger into disappointment and resignation. His Vietnam vet friend Walter, an Eight with a flashbang temper, will have none of that, though. He refocuses the Dude's anger from the rug toward the other Jeffrey Lebowski, a millionaire in town, insisting that The Dude go pay his name twin a visit and demand reimbursement for the lost rug.

Not only is Walter a hilarious character, but he's crucial to getting this story going. Nines tend to take on the energy of the people they're around, which is one of the reasons they're so good at finding common ground. They can feel where the other person is coming from. In this case, though, The Dude is imbued with the aggression of Walter's Eight, which is what catapults him into the mess he spends the rest of the movie trying to get out of (it helps that The Dude is more of a 9w8 than a 9w1). Without Walter's Eight-ness bleeding over into The Dude's psyche, he would likely ruminate on his lost rug for a few more days before shoving down his feelings about it and moving on. It's okay and often necessary when writing a Nine protagonist to have some big personalities around them from which they can siphon energy.

When The Dude goes to meet the other Jeffrey Lebowski, he's subjected to insult after insult. Rather than firmly standing up for himself, he does what Nines often do, which is to remain mostly cool in the moment (gotta maintain that harmony) and then do something passive-aggressive afterward. In this case, The Dude swipes one of Jeffrey Lebowski's rugs on his way out of the mansion.

From this point on in the story, The Dude doesn't need to do much to keep the action and conflict moving. Instead, everything seems to happen *to him*. This is fine, and typical of a Nine arc. As a real circus of characters parade by him in each scene, we see a typical Nine underreaction to some pretty fucked-up stuff. He leans on the defense mechanism of the Nine, narcotization, and smokes pot to deal with the conflict and intensity of his experience.

One can't stay asleep to anger and conflict forever, though, and we see The Dude reach his breaking point a couple of times with Walter as the weight of the shitshow they're in breaks through The Dude's fog and he moves toward his stress type of Six, catastrophizing and freaking out. He quickly returns to his normal, understated self, though.

As he yells at Walter over the phone, he finishes with the line, "Leave me the fuck alone!" then adds, "Yeah, I'll be at [bowling] practice." Even when he's furious, he's not actually willing to create lingering disconnection.

Nines like to feel the underlying connections in the world that hold everything together. The fear of being cut off or separated relates to the harmony they need to feel between themselves and others, as well as themselves and the larger world and *within* themselves. Because they perceive conflict to be the biggest irritant of their core fear, they avoid it at all costs, and if they can't avoid it, they aim their attention at de-escalating it and restoring harmony as soon as possible (sometimes before the underlying conflict is truly resolved).

Once The Dude is catapulted by Walter's intensity into the middle of a situation that's way more complicated than he expected, he spends the rest of the movie trying to resolve the conflict as simply as possible. He does run into some internal resistance, as his strong Eight wing doesn't like people telling him what to do, and Nines can be stubborn in their own right, digging their heels in when they genuinely don't like or trust the other person.

To a Nine focusing on harmony, the world seems full of ham-fisted, pugnacious people. This is a result of the Nine rejecting their own anger, aggression, and rough edges and "othering" them to keep them at arm's length. *I'm not creating conflict, that's all of* them *out there doing it*. This is a mental maneuver each type does, but the result for the Nine is that they're not sure why everyone is making such a big deal out of everything. It's difficult for them to consider the possibility that they're not making a *big enough* deal out of things.

We see The Dude bring this mentality into the threats he receives, with iconic quotes like, "Yeah? Well, you know, that's just like, uh, your opinion, man," in response to his bowling rival saying, "We're gonna fuck you up." The Nine, in their attempt to stay connected, can jump into other people's perspectives, and The Dude uses this as his defense. "That's just your opinion," is his way of denying the reality of danger presented by such threats. It's just a different point of view, not a threat from, say, a maniac pedophile that requires some kind of action.

Sometimes this approach works to de-escalate (or at least not escalate), but sometimes it pisses people off. Either way, this softening of reality is a result of The Dude's desire to avoid being cut off from the universe in a messy situation where bad people are literally cutting off toes. Tuning out reality doesn't have to be effective for him to keep using it as a strategy.

The Dude shows us the well of aggression that lives dormant inside of Nines and the lengths they will go to keep it at bay. But it always gets out, and if they don't learn to integrate it and take back the reins, it can lead them straight into the conflict they are trying so hard to avoid. For The Dude, it was never about the rug that really tied the room together. It was always about returning to a comfortable place where he could believe conflict didn't exist in his life. Through all the chaos, the death of his friend, innumerable crimes, and the imminent threat of death to himself, The Dude manages to mostly stand firm in his own chill. By the end of the film, he's able to restore that sense of harmony to his life (ignoring the rubble) as he returns to the bowling alley. It's not perfect, but it's good enough, and The Dude abides.

TYPE 1

TYPE NAMES

The Reformer, the Perfectionist, the Idealist Perspective, the Strict Perfectionist, the Improver, the Teacher, the Crusader, the Organizer, the Moralist

CORE MOTIVATIONS

Fear: of being bad, wrong, corrupt

Desire: to be good, right, and have integrity

The motivations of the One don't necessitate any sort of religious affiliation. Ones will have a strong sense of the "right" way to do things, though. They find it almost impossible to do something they consider "wrong" or "incorrect" (however they've learned to define that). The One yearns for the hit of relief that comes with thoughts, feelings, and actions they consider "good" or "right."

BRIEF DESCRIPTION

The One is arguably the most idealistic of the types, which makes them a visionary for a better world ... whatever they consider "better" to mean. They have an ability to see how the world is and then spot the distance between that and what would be better. Their deep goodness, which they tend to overlook in themselves even as they're desperate to feel like a good person, drives them to dedicate themselves to "fixing" what they don't believe is up to their high standards. This could look like trying to improve themselves, their closest friends and family, or even the world at large.

Ones will often exert themselves in the pursuit of the ideal to the point of exhaustion. Many Ones believe *not* living in a state of exhaustion shows a moral failing when there is still so much to fix. This drive comes from their terror that they may secretly be bad and wrong themselves, that they are not "good daughters," "good citizens," "good parents," and so forth. When this fear is allowed to grow unchallenged, the One turns into the nitpicker, the critic, the perfectionist, or even the punitive zealot, but you can see how this all stems from the fear that they are bad, and the overcompensation comes from their desire, if they can't achieve their own sense of perfection, to be *less* bad than others by comparison.

Because the One's fear of being bad, wrong, or corrupt is stronger than even their will to avoid physical harm, you may find them leading movements against unjust authorities, speaking their conscience even when it's unpopular, and remaining within their integrity even when it would, say, benefit their financial situation not to.

221

Ones make great friends because they are incredibly responsible and prioritize honesty and straightforwardness, even when it may make others unhappy with them in the present moment to hear it. When a One is unhealthy, they may offer criticism freely. When they are healthy, they're a source of deep wisdom and discretion.

WINGS

1w9

The Nine wing can temper some of the sharpness and criticism of the One by opening them up to more perspectives and inviting in a sense that most things progress in their own time, meaning the world may not fall apart if the One makes a mistake. Ones have a tendency to hunker down in their view of right and wrong, but the Nine wing can soften that need so that the One is able to imagine outside their own perception. On the other hand, the Nine wing can encourage the already self-depriving One to fall asleep to their own needs even more, and cause them to suppress their urges, stifling purposeful action. The 1w9 may begin to conflate purposeful action with conflict-free action and struggle to get started on the things that matter to them.

The Nine wing helps the One consider that maybe their judgment of the world isn't a final verdict. They tend to be more reserved as a result and want to think through things from multiple perspectives before taking the action their gut is shouting at them to take. If they're not careful, this can lead to a dead end, because they're asking the Thinking Center to do work that only the Action Center is qualified to do. They may miss the moment for the action and will be quite hard on themselves afterward for the inaction.

1w2

The Two wing guides the One toward a more social focus, tempering the judgment and criticism of the One with the compassion of the Two. The Two also offers the One a clear path toward goodness: service toward others. 1w2s are happy to follow this path and its promise of relief from the fear that they are bad at their core. On the other hand, this wing can amplify the existing savior complex of a One who feels like it's their responsibility to fix anything and everything they see that isn't "right." With the social justice bent of this combo, the selfless Two wing can lead the exertion-focused One straight into massive burnout and depression, when they feel impotent in the face of so many broken systems and people whom they cannot possible save.

The Two wing pulls the One toward the Feeling Center, where compassion can be found, not just for others, but for oneself. The One benefits greatly from the touch of compassion amidst the flood of self-criticism they dish up and can begin to talk back to the inner critic who rules their thoughts. The Two wing also pushes the One to be more extroverted in that their action is initiated by the needs of others, even if that service may rock the boat. On the other hand, the Two's denial of their own needs can combine with the One's fear of their natural urges to create a self-denying machine that doesn't turn off until the gears jam and the whole thing melts down.

LEVELS OF DEVELOPMENT

Healthy: Possesses wisdom, conducts oneself with integrity, "walks the walk," works toward building a better world, stands up for what they believe in despite personal cost, inspires others to be more compassionate and less judgmental, self-accepting.

Average: Striving hard worker, focuses on fixing what isn't "right," self-controlled but often rigid, critical and judgmental of self and others, functions on basis of personal obligation.

Unhealthy: Self-righteous and condemning, obsessed with wrongness of the world and others, hypocritical with incoherent moral beliefs, a sense of entitlement to punish others, downright merciless.

VICE

The One's vice is **Anger**. This presents as a dissatisfaction with reality as it falls short of their ideal for what it should be. As they hold up what is against what should be, they see the never-ending work ahead of them and can become resentful that others aren't working toward "fixing" the world and themselves to match that ideal. The vice is also directed internally for the One, as they become frustrated with their own shortfalls, even as they view Anger itself as an imperfection that must be corrected.

Your Type 1 character will get themselves into trouble by trying to fix what they think is broken without ample consideration of whose toes they step on (or that it may not need fixing to begin with). Their resentment, frustration, and criticism will drive away the people they need the most.

VIRTUE

The virtue of the One is **Serenity**. Only once the One accepts that their ideal might not be *the* ideal in any universal way can they experience the state of Serenity. As the One lets go of the urge to "fix" what doesn't meet their individual idea of perfection, they can appreciate that everything is already perfectly imperfect and enjoy sitting back to appreciate the intricate workings of the world that existed before they were born and will exist long after they've passed away.

STRESS TYPE

Moves toward Four. When their efforts toward doing things "right" don't lead to the desired outcomes, they can start to wonder what the point of trying so hard and wearing themselves down into nubs even is. They slide toward the melancholy, brooding, and rumination of the Four, withdrawing emotionally from others and feeling generally misunderstood. As their connection to their sense of purpose frays, the One can slip into nihilism. If handled with care and support, that nihilism can be a liberating force that shows the One there isn't ONE correct way to be, and they do, in fact, get to design a purposeful life that they enjoy living.

GROWTH TYPE

As the One lets go of the idea that everything must be purposeful and well organized to be good, they gain access to more moments of humor, spontaneity, and joy from their growth type, the Seven. They stop making decisions based on obligation and discover that their purpose is buoyed rather than sunk by a sense of lightness and enjoyment.

COMMON THEME PAIRINGS

Truth, justice, righteousness, fairness, courage, good/evil, responsibility, corruption, honesty, trust

TRIAD/CENTER

Body/Gut/Action

Ones have a strong gut instinct and are incredibly intuitive, honing their perception around the intentions of others. Does this person care about others? Are they a good person? Is there a darkness hovering around them?

This can make Ones a strong judge of character as long as they don't fall into their common trap of needing to justify every gut instinct in their head before allowing themselves to take action. This justification process often makes Ones look like they belong in the Head/Thinking/Cognitive triad, but the One's justification *rarely* increases the accuracy of their intuition. In fact, it usually dulls it and prevents the One from taking the action their gut is telling them to take, creating an exhausting internal tension.

On the other hand, if the One hasn't deconstructed their learned biases and developed beyond black-and-white thinking, they may mistake bias and prejudice for a gut instinct. A One who has done some of that work and begins to trust their intuition rather than getting blocked by needing to justify themselves often appears to possess a supernatural ability to get a read on the intentions of others.

Anger/Control/Autonomy

Ones don't tend to think of themselves as angry people and resent those who say they are. Most ones consider showing anger to be a bad thing and therefore internalize the emotion, turning it against themselves through the use of an inner critic whose tempting lie is that the anger will help steer them toward perfection.

In this way, the Ones tend to first aim their need for control at themselves in various ways. They need to "act right," "think right," "emote right," even "look right," to the point where their control over their routines and habits can become extreme and harmful to their ability to experience simple joy.

Their hope is that through controlling aspects of themselves, they can earn their autonomy from the world. If they live above reproach, they can finally live however they want. Someday.

Once the One can stop letting their frustration about the gap between reality and the ideal infiltrate every corner of their world, the anger lessens, and the One can begin to alchemize it into meaningful and righteous action when it's called for. Mostly, the One can begin to unclench their fists and relax their shoulders, recognizing that they don't have to control every aspect of their life for their life to be quite good and worthy of living fully.

INTERACTION STYLE

Ones are a **compliant** type. They try to earn the autonomy they're seeking through being right and perfect. They feel like they must "deserve" something before they allow themselves to have it, and often assume that the misfortune they face is also somehow earned.

DIALOGUE

The idealism of the One shows through in their speech, with lots of "shoulds" and "shouldn'ts." "They shouldn't do that," "It shouldn't be this hard," "No one should have to suffer that way." Because the way Ones sort the world is right/wrong and good/bad, you'll hear lots of those adjectives find their way into dialogue as well: "You're sorting the clothes wrong," or "We can't let the bad guys win."

The One's tendency toward justification may also show up in dialogue, as they feel the need to explain *why* they're doing what they're doing, and how it's for the best. They may also demand that others explain themselves in this way, concerned that they might accidentally sign on to something that leaves them with no morally pure choice moving forward.

Lastly, if you're writing a less likeable One, be sure to include criticism of others. Anxiety in Ones tends to take the form of judgment and criticism, and that will spill out in their dialogue. Sometimes it'll be passing a moral judgment, like, "They're not a good person," and sometimes it'll be more nitpicky, like, "You always leave the lights on. Are you trying to kill the planet?"

STEREOTYPES

The One is often stereotyped as the Type A anal retentive who must have everything in its place and who makes everyone around them walk on eggshells or fear their harsh judgment. The reason they're stereotyped this way is because, yeah, it's common for the core motivations to express themselves this way. But this isn't a given, especially as the One becomes healthier.

Ones can be sloppy, just like everyone else. Check the closets of their house. Better yet, drop by their house unannounced and see what it looks like (they will likely hate you for doing this). There's also a subtype of One (the Social One) who is more focused on improving systems, nudging them toward fairness and justice, than keeping things neat and tidy in their environment.

The One is also frequently stereotyped as being rigid and not a lot of fun. While that can certainly be the case for some Ones most of the time, it's important to remember that Ones make great satirists, as they often develop a sense of humor to soften the blows their inner critic hurls their way (some of the internal harassment is truly something only a cartoon villain would say to anyone; it's so mean). Nothing like seeing how things are a mess to be able to critique in a humorous way. Ones are also deeply sensitive and crave joyful moments that will elevate them out of the morass of their moralistic thinking.

EASY MISTAKES TO MAKE

Ones are not rule *followers* so much as rule *makers*. They will follow rules that make sense to them, but they are generally game to break rules that they think are unjust or unnecessary. Meanwhile, in a chaotic environment, the Ones tend to be the first to call a timeout and start establishing the rules for those involved. Their rules will generally be focused on fairness, ethics, and order.

Ones default to black-and-white thinking, but as characters, they really shine in stories where there is no clear right or wrong option available. Once they get over their initial disgust over not having an obvious morally pure choice, they can become an expert at determining the "most right" thing to do.

EXAMPLES

Atticus Finch (*To Kill a Mockingbird*), Batman (*The Batman*, 2024), Hermione Grainger (Harry Potter), Elsa (Disney's *Frozen*), Claire Fraser (*Outlander*), Monica Geller (*Friends*), Ned Stark (A Song of Ice and Fire), Claude Frollo (*The Hunchback of Notre Dame*), Eli Sunday (*There Will Be Blood*)

DEEP DIVE: ELSA

I searched high and low for an interesting example of a Type 1 that most people would have familiarity with but also wasn't the stereotypical anal-retentive control freak or self-righteous crusader that's commonly depicted. In my experience, authors tend to have a pretty firm grasp of the stereotypical One, but often miss what's happening beneath the self-disciplined exterior. Ones aren't simple by any means, and beneath the placid surface there's a storm of an inner world. That's why I thought Elsa from Disney's Frozen *was a fantastic example of showing the deep waters beneath the icy exterior of the One.*

Analysis: At the start of the movie, we see two sisters, Anna and Elsa, playing together as little kids do. They're carefree, imaginative, and hold nothing back. They see nothing wrong with the fun they're having as they play around in their castle in the far-north Kingdom of Arendelle.

One slight complication, though: Elsa has magical powers that allow her to shoot snow and ice from her hands. However, as the sisters play together, this is considered a perk and part of their play. Everything that is natural to them is integrated into the play.

Then Elsa makes a mistake, as children (and all people) do, and the result is that she hits Anna with the winter powers while trying to create a snow mound. Anna is gravely injured from the blast, and we see her red hair marked with a white streak in a visual manifestation and perpetual reminder of Elsa's mistake.

Their parents, the king and queen, rush in and see that Elsa has hurt her sister, and the family rushes down to visit the trolls for help. The trolls heal Anna and wipe her memory of Elsa's magic as a way of trying to keep everyone safe from these "dangerous" powers. Elsa is instructed to keep her magic hidden from then on. Her parents lock her away in the castle, separating her from her loving and playful sister.

At this point, every One watching is crying a little bit. The story so far is the story that every One carries in their heart:

231

they are not allowed to make mistakes. Other people can be careless, but if the One is, people will get hurt because the One is, at their core, *bad* and *dangerous*. They cannot trust themselves to let go and have fun. Those freedoms are for *other* people. This is a wound the One carries that leads to the perfectionism, self-criticism, self-discipline, and lack of emoting that we tend to associate with the type. Early on, the One learns that self-control is the only way to protect others from their perceived innate wrongness.

It's important to note that nobody in Elsa's family thought her powers needed to be suppressed until her mistake was stigmatized. The fear of imperfection (mistakes) was then reinforced with words from her parents, like, "Getting upset only makes it worse." When she becomes emotional is when she struggles the most to control her powers, so Elsa, like all Ones, learns that emotions are dangerous. Emotions cause chaos that leads to devastating mistakes.

The One focuses much of their attention on not being the cause of harm. Harm is a focus of each of the types in the Action Center (8-9-1), but they take different approaches to it. The Eight, whose fear is being harmed and controlled, goes on the offensive to avoid being harmed, to the point where they sometimes harm others in preemptive self-protection. The Nine minimizes their impact on the world around them, attempting to avoid causing harm but also overlooking opportunities to prevent it. And the One turns to self-control to avoid causing harm, while believing there is something essentially violent or dangerous about themselves that must be kept locked away. The One becomes afraid of their impulses, assuming each one must be bad and dangerous. This belief is why Elsa stops trusting her natural magic, assuming that it can only hurt others.

This repressed energy takes the form of anger for the One, but it's turned toward the self. This can only last so long before the One slips and makes a mistake, and we see that happen with Elsa at the coronation day event. When Anna asks for her sister's blessing to marry a man she just met, and Elsa (wisely) says that's crazy—and no, she won't offer her blessing—Anna attempts to physically control her sister by grabbing her hand as she attempts to walk away. Elsa's glove (the mechanism that contains her powers) slips off and, as with any pressure cooker, that's all it takes for the One's self-focused aggression to spill over into the external world. Elsa reveals her magic not only to her sister, but to all the guests inside. Elsa directs only a tiny portion of the iciness that she's lived with all these years at others. The secret's out, and it's a scandal.

Ones reach their limit eventually, and the harshness (iciness) they direct at themselves reaches a breaking point. Eruptions of anger are common when this happens. It's a quick and biting lashing out, a flash point. And then the shame that the One has developed around being angry comes flooding in and the self-recrimination voiced by their inner critic clamors louder than ever. *My anger is bad. My anger is dangerous.* This is usually when we see them slip into their stress type of Four.

And that's exactly what Elsa does after the public display. She flees the castle, even though she's now the queen, and finds an isolated mountaintop where she can "let it go." This mimics the move from the contained and repressed One toward the expressive but withdrawn Four. Since Elsa can't hold her natural impulses back anymore, she finds a safe place to retreat to, where she can fully express who she is without fear of harming others.

The song "Let It Go" is a wonderful embodiment of what happens in stress for the One after the initial sting of shame wears off. They can use that moment to reconnect with the parts of themselves they've learned to fear. They can be messy and not worry about how their mistakes will cause harm. We see Elsa break through to this new experience when she proclaims that "the perfect girl is gone."

Up on that mountaintop of freedom, Elsa creates a castle for herself. It feels good, but ultimately, she would be lonely if she spent the rest of her life there. It also doesn't resolve the deeper problem: her forced separation from her sister Anna, who represents the part of herself she had to shut off to "be good."

We get a glimpse of what Elsa needs for a happy ending when she loses control in her castle and tells herself, "Conceal it, don't feel it." The image accompanying that shows her surrounded by a bunch of pointy icicles aimed at her; a hostile, self-created environment to keep herself caged so that others don't pay the price.

Elsa's focus on self-control and her movement *away* from others fails to acknowledge what is lost when she does this. Throughout the story, she repeatedly draws the same lesson from events: her emotions are dangerous, her heart presents a danger, and the only way to show love is through self-control, through not showing any emotions at all. This is common for Ones, who forget to question their staunch belief that their natural self is bad, wrong, and dangerous, and that the passion and play others enjoy safely isn't an indulgence the One can afford. They wrap their heart in ice as a means of showing their love to others through self-restraint.

This is a poor solution to the problem, as Elsa discovers toward the end of the movie when Anna sacrifices herself to save her sister. Only then does Elsa realize what she's lost through her ineffective approach. Her self-control shatters, and she throws her arms around her sister's frozen body, letting her heart out of its cage, letting her natural emotions in the moment spring forth. Through that process, Elsa does the thing she didn't think she was able to do: thaw what's frozen. Her heart was never the problem after all; it was the solution.

We often assume that Ones are always moralists or activists, and sometimes that's accurate, especially if they have a strong Two wing. But the fear of being bad, wrong, or corrupt that the One feels tends to be applied strongly to their emotions. Ones struggle to trust that they'll show the "right" emotion in the moment, so they show nothing at all. This earns female Ones especially the label of "ice queen" at some point in their life. For male Ones, we usually hear the descriptor "stoic."

Elsa is literally an ice queen. And like most metaphorical ice queens, she was taught early on to believe that she was responsible for her emotions rather than being responsible for the actions associated with those emotions. Emotions simply happen, and we have very little say in them. Ones feel like they need to control that initial emotional response, though, that simply *feeling* something like anger is dangerous. But emotions aren't dangerous or bad.

Unfortunately, the belief that experiencing "bad" emotions is evidence that one is naturally bad or corrupt gets lodged in the One's psyche early on, and it's reinforced every time they experience one of those "bad" emotions that could inspire them to take harmful action. Taking responsibility for one's behavior is great, but trying to take responsibility for the emotional response before it's ever led to anything is where the One trips up.

Early on in the movie, the trolls ask a crucial question: *Are Elsa's powers natural or the result of a curse?* This is not a throwaway line. We learn that Elsa was born with this power. She later interprets this as being born "wrong," which is a typical, ungenerous One interpretation, and in deciding this, she blocks herself from the possibility that her powers might be important for her purpose and calling.

The One may begin to assume that every impulse they experience must be bad. They employ the defense mechanism of reaction formation against this, assuming that as long as they do the opposite of their natural urge, they'll be acting in goodness and rightness. If they have the urge to eat something sweet, then it's obviously time for some spinach. If they feel the urge to express themselves, then the right thing to do is to reject that impulse and listen to others more. We see this big time in Elsa. When she feels the urge to connect with her sister through the shut doors, she instead chooses to pull back, making herself even more unavailable.

This rejection of impulses doesn't live only in the heart, but also in the gut. The One is a gut type, after all, but they disconnect from their body and instinctive knowledge, believing their instincts are bad and dangerous. As we saw when Elsa refused to bless her sister's engagement to a man she'd only just met (and who is later revealed to be a manipulator), Elsa's instincts are actually dead-on. The line between being judgmental and showing sound judgment can be razor thin for a One, but in this moment, we see the latter show up. Elsa's intuition is good, if she'll just listen to it.

In the end, her sister's show of love is enough to break down Elsa's barriers. Her heart is set free, and her urge to embrace her sister wins out over her fear and all the false lessons it's taught her. Letting go of the fear's lies is ultimately what is needed, but also the way for the deep and true goodness living inside of Elsa to spring forth and restore rightness to the world, melting the snow all around her.

BEYOND DOMINANT TYPE

OTHER CHARACTER CONSIDERATIONS

In this section, we'll explore some of the complications in the writing process. But if you find yourself feeling overwhelmed by all you *could* take into consideration for your characters, I encourage you to take a deep breath and a step back, and simply refocus your attention on the core motivations of the type. That will get you ninety percent of the way. Come back to this section later as needed.

Let's dig in to what other influences will keep our characters from looking totally and precisely like a single, dominant (stereo)type (not to mention, we all technically have each of the types inside us to various degrees, but let's not let all those horses out of the barn yet).

Just like you and me, our characters are, after all, learning from a very young age how to fit in with others of different types who may have more power and conflicting values. Outside influences certainly show up in us, regardless of how much we may want to believe we cannot be influenced. It's crucial to consider the external factors that may become internalized and then appear in our iconic characters.

241

PERSONAL HISTORY

Two characters of the same Enneagram type can show up incredibly differently on the page. This is great news because it means we don't have to start copy-pasting characters as soon as we have more than nine.

One of the reasons this is possible is because the personal history of each character colors how the core fear and desire express themselves through thoughts, feelings, and behaviors.

Imagine you have two characters, let's call them Helga and Renata.

Helga grew up in a home where there was often not enough to eat for weeks at a time. Her parents each worked two jobs, which left her and her siblings alone to fend for themselves most of their waking hours.

Renata, an only child, was born into wealth, raised mostly by a nanny and a private tutor, and had two diplomat parents who carted her around the world as more of a trophy than a human being.

Now let's say both Helga and Renata are Threes (core fear: being worthless or lacking value).

How might their different experiences growing up make this Three manifest in different ways?

Here are some of my guesses...

Helga

- Helga may believe that to be *valuable*, you must *provide* for those around you.
- If Helga's parents were emotionally neglectful or rejecting in those sparse moments when they were around, she may not respect her parents because their hard work didn't create the monetary value needed to keep their kids fed.
- If Helga received love and attention from her parents in those sparse moments when they were around, she might grow up to believe that a person's worth *isn't* defined by their wealth. She might use her personal achievements as a way of shining light on this for the rest of the world.

Renata

- Renata may believe that what people in positions of high status think about you determines your value.
- Renata may believe that her worthiness is wrapped up in how she looks, her politeness, and her academic success. (In other words, how her *performance* is judged by others.)
- Renata may live a life of pursuing career goals that

her parents would approve of, forgetting to ask herself what she'd actually like to be doing.

You can see how the details of these two characters' early childhoods influence how their core motivations are likely to manifest.

It seems unlikely that Renata would use her personal achievements as a way of highlighting wealth inequality and deconstructing the idea that people who are wealthier work harder than those who are not, as Helga might. Renata doesn't have the background to support her motivations showing up that way.

Now, let's pretend that both Helga and Renata—same backgrounds as before—are Sixes (core fear: lacking support and guidance).

How might those same experiences in childhood make this Six express in adulthood?

Here are some of my guesses:

Helga

- Helga works a stable government job and puts half of her income into a savings account. She doesn't trust the stock market, as it's designed to serve the rich, not people like her. She currently has a year's worth of expenses saved, but she's hoping to get that up to two.
- If Helga is married, she's found a confident go-getter, perhaps a bold and confident Eight with a high-paying job, and who she knows would go to prison to keep her safe.

- Then again, it's equally possible she married a slacker who can't hold a job and who relies on her too much to ever leave her. By providing for both herself and her spouse, she's repeating the familiar patterns of responsibility she once had regarding her siblings, recreating the scene while trying to produce a more stable financial outcome than before.

Renata

- Renata is a financial advisor to the wealthy. She works as a sane counterbalance and a voice of reason to the reckless spending the ultrawealthy can get away with. Her childhood taught her how to cozy up to big egos, and she's dedicated much of her life to keeping these idiots from going bankrupt. In return, they're loyal customers.
- If Renata is married, she's found someone who doesn't care much about keeping up appearances as her parents did and would rather spend a cozy night inside on the couch (perhaps a Nine [core fear: being cut off and separate] or Two [core fear: being unloved and unwanted]).
- Then again, it's equally possible that Renata has married a flashy, high-status partner who plays the same games as her parents did. In this way, Renata attempts to earn the emotional support her parents never offered through her spouse. Is it working? Tune in next week …

The influences of personal history and the way the type manifests in your character stems almost entirely from early childhood, particularly the character's relationship (or lack thereof) with their caretakers.

But specific traumas can also inform the expression of the type. And what's traumatic to one type might be water off the back of another. That depends on how the situation unfolds and pokes at one's existing core fear.

For instance, let's say Benji is held up at gunpoint, but is himself armed and shoots and kills the would-be robber. While, yes, he might be rattled *regardless* of type, we might see that his action either affirms or conflicts with his sense of self, *depending* on his type.

If Benji's an Eight (core fear: being harmed or controlled), this situation might *affirm* his sense that he's strong and powerful. In that way, it might not be something that settles in him as trauma.

But if Benji is a Nine (core fear: being cut off and separate), shooting and killing someone, even someone pointing a gun at him, might *conflict* strongly with his sense that he's a peaceful person. The situation may be incredibly traumatic because it's hitting at his identity. To a conflict-averse person, murder is the definition of trauma—too much, too fast, too soon.

Another example: Imagine we have Marco, a Three (core fear: lacking worth or value), who's going into his boss's office expecting to be promoted to partner but is instead fired for failing to disclose a perceived conflict of interest. Suddenly, Marco is not only bereft of the job that supported his lavish lifestyle, but his reputation in his industry is now mud. His sense that he's successful, which is crucial to a Three, would be stabbed right in the heart. The moment would surely be traumatic, which would, frankly, make this a tremendous inciting incident for his character arc.

Meanwhile, if Marco is a Seven (core fear: being trapped in pain and deprivation), there may be a twinge of pain accompanying the blindside, but maybe he was thinking of changing careers anyway (as Sevens often do). He doesn't feel the sting of shame in this scenario nearly as much as he can taste the sweetness of freedom and possibility. It would take a lot of setup on the part of the author to make this a truly traumatic experience for Marco, and so it doesn't create quite as potent of an inciting incident for the Seven as opposed to the Three.

As authors, it's our responsibility, our duty, our perverse pleasure, to figure out effective personal histories for our characters that allow us to torment them in just the right way.

It's possible to get lost in the weeds a bit when it comes to personal histories, so just remember that the character's personal history filters through the motivations to create the particular expression of their type, as you saw with Helga and Renata.

OVERLAYS

Overlays are expectations from others that a character absorbs by osmosis, as a result of being part of that group. To remain included and okay, they must learn the play the game of a type that may not be their own.

For example, a Two (core fear: to be unworthy of love) subjected to a Seven (core fear: to be trapped in pain or deprivation) overlay must learn how to be *helpful* (the focus of the Two) in a way that doesn't make others feel *trapped* (the fear of the Seven) by the obligation of reciprocation. The Two may also focus their *help* on making others *feel good* (the focus of the Seven) more so than anything else. The Two may "help" others by reminding them to *sublimate* (the defense mechanism of the Seven) their unpleasant feelings —silver-line them immediately, that is—rather than sit with painful feelings to process them, because that's the game the Two believes they must play to be worthy of love within that Seven overlay.

Let's look at some other common overlays that may

influence the way your character goes about avoiding their fear and pursuing their desire.

FAMILY OF ORIGIN

It's difficult to be an author without also dabbling in attachment styles and family systems. Because so much of the expression of an Enneagram type is developed early in life, the first adults we learn from play a big role in how that's expressed. Whether your character was raised by their biological parents, grandparents, aunts, foster parents, or nuns, this will shape how their type expresses itself. Note that this will not *determine* what type they are, or else siblings from the same household would end up the same type fairly consistently, which is not the case at all.

It's common when I'm working with an author for them to feel like they might be split between two types. "I'm equal parts Five *and* One," they might say. Almost invariably, one of those types is their actual dominant type and the other is the type of one of their parents. If they're torn between being a One (core fear: being bad and corrupt) or a Five (core fear: being incompetent or incapable), after some exploration, they may discover that they're a One who has learned to equate being intellectual and unemotional with being good, because intelligence was positively reinforced by their Five parent.

Sometimes people will say, "Of course I'm a Two. I was the oldest child and had to take care of my siblings." In my experience, birth order doesn't play much of a role, if any, in determining type. For instance, I've worked with Sevens who were the oldest child, and when their parents put them in charge of their siblings, the Sevens got the hell out of the house as soon as they could. The unmet parental expectations may still linger in the Seven's psyche ("I'm so irresponsible"), but that doesn't make the Seven suddenly able to sit in the pain and deprivation required to be a child responsible for other children.

PARTNERSHIPS

Partnerships also create overlays. This could be a business partnership, a roommate relationship, or a marriage. You'll see this a lot in long-term marriages, as each person takes on more of their partner's patterns to be able to cohabitate and understand one another. However, some types will take on much more of their partner than others. Nines, Twos, Threes, Fours, and Sixes are more likely to adopt the overlay of their partners than Ones, Fives, Sevens, and Eights. That's not to say that the Ones, Fives, Sevens, and Eights are inflexible and above influence, only that those types tend to have stronger pushback against influence.

When considering how your character might be influenced by an overlay within their partnership, it's important to start with what type the character is and what type their partner is. It can require more than a surface-level understanding of each type to imagine how the influence would play out. For instance, how would a Two-Six pairing play out? In this case, the two types would likely meet somewhere close to the middle, with the Two (core fear: being unwanted and unloved) learning to be *helpful* by calming the Six's anxieties and showing up reliably, as a Six might. Then the Six (core fear: lacking support or guidance) might use their powers of *prediction* to anticipate what help the Two needs but won't ask for, as a Two might. In this way, the Two and Six adapt to each other while doing it in their own way.

That being said, this shared influence doesn't always happen in partnerships, and if it doesn't, the partnership might not last.

Consider a Nine and an Eight in a partnership. The bold and often inflexible Eight (core fear: being harmed or controlled), who prides herself on rejecting influence, is less likely to show signs of a Nine overlay than the flexible and accommodating Nine (core fear: being separate and cut off) is of showing signs of an Eight overlay. They could certainly learn a lot from each other, but over time, if the Eight keeps rejecting the Nine's influence, it's likely that the Nine will disappear completely and the Eight will start to feel contempt for what they perceive to be the Nine's weakness of personality.

GENDER AND SEXUAL ORIENTATION

Gender expectations, which we all internalize to varying degrees even if we don't naturally or intentionally conform to them, dictate the "allowable" ways a character's type may be expressed through thoughts, feelings, and behaviors.

Of course, gender expectations are not set in stone, because as much as some would attribute them to "biology," that claim crumbles under only minor inspection. Gender expectations vary throughout history and from culture to culture. In present day, they may be somewhat nebulous still (by design, so that nobody can ever truly satisfy them and must keep striving), but we have a general notion that can inform us as authors.

But just because gender expectations are a societal concoction doesn't mean they aren't influencing how we and our characters show up. They hold a great deal of influence over that.

For instance, imagine a Two (core fear: being unloved and unwanted). Are you imagining a straight cisgendered man? Probably not if you were raised in the modern Western world.

So many of the common qualities of the Two—emotionally attuned, nurturing, endlessly self-sacrificing, labor taken for granted—are considered "feminine" and simply *expected* of straight cisgendered women. In this way, many women experience a Two overlay brought on by societal gender expectations.

And here's the kicker: if the woman is actually a Two, then her unhealthy patterns of giving beyond what she has to give, putting everyone else first, and never throwing up clear boundaries are *socially rewarded*! That means she'll face even *more* resistance in her work to liberate herself from these patterns because she's being offered the (delicious) empty calories of praise and lots of conditional love in return for continuing her unhealthy patterns. That's a lot to give up to pursue unconditional love that the Two may not even know exists.

If you're wondering, yes, there are straight cisgendered men who are Twos. Go ahead and scratch your head at how that might express itself in a society that claims emotionally attuned men aren't "real" men. Think of how many people still turn their nose up at the idea of a male nurse, and you'll start to see how gender overlays can have a major impact on a character's psyche.

What types are more often reserved for those who identify as straight men? Three, Five, and Eight jump out to me, but not necessarily the healthy versions of those. The ambitious, efficient, and competitive Three may be perceived to be "manly" just as the emotionless, clinical, and "objective" Five may also be an acceptable iteration. And then there's the strong, powerful, bullying Eight who believes sweat is weakness leaving the body, a caricature of masculinity that we see posted all over social media as aspirational for any "real" man.

Meanwhile, women who are Eights can expect a life of people trying to "put them in their place" and "not ask for so much."

Wherever your character falls in their gender identity and sexual orientation, you'll find the full range of dominant types available to you. There's no correlation between being a trans man and being a particular Enneagram type, for instance. But the overlay of gender expectations will still be present in the character's psyche.

It may be that you're writing in a world with different gender expectations from what you and most of your readers grew up with. That's totally fine. Make it clear that in this universe, women are expected to be the strongest or most intelligent, and men are considered the caretakers. Or do away with the binary completely! You'll have to establish that clearly in the text, though, because readers will be bringing their own gender overlays with them into that first page and may become confused. In my publishing experience, there's little that is more ruthlessly protected by the average reader than internalized gender expectations. You can set people off in the most tremendous ways by simply poking at these roles a little in your manuscript. If you've ever gotten a "the female MC was unlikeable" comment, you know what I mean.

That's why recognizing that the overlay of gender expectations is always present for both the characters and the readers is so important. I'm not telling you to adhere to the expectations that you were born into and didn't consent to at any point. In fact, creating a character that pushes back against these gender overlays is a fantastic way to make them stand out to readers and become, you guessed it, iconic.

Note: Because gay men are often considered "feminine" by society, your gay character may also take on an overlay of a Two, even if they aren't one. Similarly, lesbians who are considered more "masculine" by society may take on overlays of types that are more "socially acceptable" for men, like Three, Five, and Eight. What overlay might your nonbinary character take on? And here we run straight into the constraints of gender expectations, folks. Our ideas about gender are all made up, but that doesn't mean they don't matter to your character, the story world, and the reader.

Asking yourself how your own ideas of gender may be influencing what types you assign to your characters is always a fruitful exploration for an author.

CULTURAL

Cultural overlays play a huge role if you're writing characters from various ethnic backgrounds. A person's culture informs how their family of origin might look, what they expect from partnerships, and their expectations surrounding gender. But their culture may also have other influences like spiritual or religious stories that shape it, histories of being oppressed or being oppressors, long-term systems of government, established social hierarchies, and economic systems. All of these create type overlays that may reward people of the same type as the overlay or punish those with a different type.

For instance, the economic system of capitalism has a Three overlay. It's a game of generating monetary worth and value, sometimes at the expense of everything else and to the point of exploiting labor, which is where it gets a little icky. But culture isn't static. If you look back at the time of the robber barons in the U.S., one might argue that it *wasn't* a time of capitalism with its Three overlay, but rather a time of lustful conquering and massive power imbalances, which leans more toward an overlay of (unhealthy) Eight.

Different countries have different cultural overlays, as well. Germany has a One overlay, Canada has a Nine overlay, France has a Four overlay, and so on. Yes, this is painting with a broad brush, and there are certainly subcultures within each of these that don't follow along. But it's important, as an author, to consider these layers of overlay for our characters. Are you writing that character like a One intentionally, or are you intuitively adding some One-ness because they're from Germany and your mind intuitively connects the two?

Cultural overlays can easily turn into unhealthy stereotypes about members of a particular culture, so we don't need to overdo them. We can simply hold them loosely in our minds as we write a character, allowing them to inform but not become the entirety of our character's expression.

This is especially true when we write characters of different races from our own. Do you understand the cultural overlay and how the character is rewarded or punished by it? Do you understand the flow of power in the society and where your character falls in the social hierarchies? Is that character you're creating really a bold Eight (core fear: being harmed and controlled), or is she simply a Black woman in America whose joy, success, and integrity are in natural opposition to established power structures and therefore perceived as a challenge to the way society has been structured? (Black women in America are often mistyped [generally by white practitioners] as Eights for this very reason.)

As with gender expectations, cultural overlays are helpful to consider in crafting your iconic character. Not only will it keep you from committing all kinds of accidental faux pas created by your own lens and cultural biases, but it will help you better understand the richness of your iconic character and what cultural baggage they (and you and the readers) may be carrying around. We all have it, so let's practice naming it.

SKILLS & STRENGTHS

The Enneagram alone won't tell us what skills a character holds. There's no correlation between Fives and mental math, for instance. While Fours are incredibly creative and expressive, that doesn't mean that they're all strong visual artists. Not every One has the spatial skills to reorganize a pantry for maximum order.

We're each born with particular innate talents, and those don't necessarily line up nice and neat with our Enneagram type, which is what allows every human to be so different from every other human. There's an infinite number of combinations available.

It can be interesting to imagine how, say, a Six (core fear: lacking support or guidance) might behave if they're born with a strong sense of smell versus being born *without* that sense entirely. How might their tendency to seek external security develop as a result? Surely, you, the highly creative author, can imagine some way to use a detail like that to add to the iconic nature of your character. Does being a "super smeller" help them look out for threats? Does lacking a sense of smell cause them to be on high alert around food? Do they have a sidekick whom they rely on for support in this way?

And how might a Six handle not having a sense of smell versus a Seven or a Two? How might the perceived setback (or what a "super smeller" like me might consider a *superpower*) interact with their core fear in interesting ways?

There are certain *learned* skills that it may make sense for a particular type to develop, but it's up to the author to connect the two with logic. Did this character learn pottery because it was a way she could feel more competent and capable (Type 5)? Or did she learn pottery because she was trying to challenge her perfectionist tendencies (Type 1)? Did he learn how to cook because he didn't trust other people to keep from tampering with his food (Type 6) (interesting backstory potential here!), or did he learn how to cook because it was an easy way to be helpful to others (Type 2)?

It's your job as an author to draw these connections between skills and talents and the character's motivation, and when you do, you create meaning from those "interesting bits" that we like to pick up from everyday life. A character with a lot of "interesting bits" about them can feel thrown together if we fail to connect those things to their core motivation in meaningful ways.

These skills and natural strengths are where you can put some unforgettable flourishes on an already interesting character to take them from well developed, coherent, and unforgettable to truly iconic.

SECTION 4: THE FIRST STEP

PUTTING KNOWLEDGE INTO ACTION

This book is designed to give you sufficient information on each type to feel a certain degree of competency in writing your characters. Even if you can't yet see all of the types in stark detail, you really only need to see the silhouette to get started, and you can refer back to the previous section to color it in.

But how do you begin to put this new knowledge into action? How do you take what you know about the Seven, say, and use that to infuse the knowledge into the pages of your novel? And how do you keep from being overwhelmed by the initial learning curve?

This section offers support for that. There are certain pieces of advice that I offer authors to help move from thinking and conceptualizing into the action of writing. I've read too many craft books that offer up a concept but don't necessarily guide authors on the best way to use it independently, so I'm not trying to create more of that frustration in the industry. I don't see any point to keeping these tips secret, since it's still up to each writer to put in the hard work of writing the book. And, frankly, as a reader myself, I would love to see more books out there with iconic characters.

So, here's my basic guidance for putting your new knowledge into action.

START SIMPLE

It's tempting for some authors to cram too much into the character before even writing the first page. This frontloading works for some people, but frequently it's the result of the author attempting to soothe their own anxieties and avoid the scary part of starting the draft rather than a tool the author actually needs.

If you haven't been using the Enneagram as a model for your characters, I assure you that by simply establishing what basic type your protagonist and antagonist are, you'll be positioning yourself wonderfully for making decisions along the way. You don't have to flesh out every character in this way before you start, and if you feel like you need to, I ask you to pause and question that feeling, because it might be a delaying tactic.

If you're still getting familiar with the types, I suggest not trying to also dig into what wing they have. Some characters (and people) don't have or need a strong wing. Following the KISS (keep it simple, silly) model is not only fine, it's perfectly sufficient for creating an iconic character.

Sometimes, authors will learn about the concept of how we have all nine types inside of us to some degree, and they'll go, "Oh great! I'll make this character a #1 Type 3 and a #2 Type 8 and a #3 Type 5 …" and then I'm forced to stage a swift intervention. You really don't need to worry about what the second-highest type is for your character. That's almost guaranteed to muddy the waters more than it adds interest and dimension, especially if you're new to using this framework.

Each of the types also has three subtypes within it (Self-Preservation, One-on-One, and Social), which I intentionally didn't get into in this book because it, too, can lead to more hand wringing from authors than clarity and ease of use. Yes, a type can look quite different from subtype to subtype, but you can also do everything you need as an author developing an iconic character without getting *that* into the weeds. It's best, when starting out, to stick with the general type descriptions and practice returning to the core motivations every time your character has a clear decision to make.

Keeping it simple is how you start. Can you make it more complicated as you become more comfortable with the framework? Of course. Some of you will hunger for that and will go look up subtype descriptions on the internet or in Enneagram books before you even finish this book. Meanwhile, others will be happy just sticking to the basic framework. Neither approach is more right or wrong than the other.

Whatever direction you take, start simple. Trust me. Sometimes the simplest use of the Enneagram creates the most iconic characters.

START WITH THE FAMILIAR

Thankfully, there is no "right" type of protagonist or antagonist for a particular genre, so you're free to pick which types you want to work with.

I suggest you start with a type that's familiar to you, one that just makes sense to you. Often, that means writing characters who share your Enneagram type. But it might also mean writing a character with the Enneagram type of your spouse, best friend, parents, or favorite fictional character.

As you read through the descriptions of the nine types, there will be certain types that just don't quite resonate with you at first (or for a while). Their perspective, their lens, is just too far outside the range of your own. I felt this way about the Six when I first started learning about the types. I had to listen to a lot of Sixes talk, read up on the type, identify a few of my close friends as the Sixes they were before it clicked for me. (One of my closest friends since high school is *definitely* a counterphobic Six, which was not only useful to my understanding of the type, but made sense of so much of his behavior, which had previously left me *baffled*.)

You can do yourself a huge favor if you just set aside the types you're struggling to wrap your head around, or keep them as secondary characters for now. It's never necessary to write a particular type of protagonist, and you're much less likely to write something iconic if you're struggling to understand how the mechanisms work.

FOCUS ON DECISION POINTS

What I would hate to see is a bunch of authors tripping themselves up in their writing because they're now worried, "Am I doing this type right?" None of this is designed to be a tool for anxiety. In fact, the whole point of the framework is to provide a reference for when you're already feeling stuck and simply need something to refer back to so that you can get writing again.

It's fine if your Eight asks a few questions outside of an interrogation room. It's not a big deal if your Four says something clichéd or follows the crowd occasionally. Those little moments likely won't even ping on the reader's radar if you nail the decision points.

That's why I suggest you focus your attention, when new to this, on those big decision points for your protagonist—particularly, the inciting incident, the midpoint, and the climax (though there may be a few others that stand out to you, and you're free to focus on those as well!). Our Enneagram type shows up most fully at the decision points in our lives. Do we remain loyal to our friends or our ideals? Do we stay quiet or speak up? And most importantly, *why?*

Letting your readers in on the motivation behind your characters' decisions is the easiest way to show their type. Keep in mind, a Seven and a Two might make the same choice as one another, but the motivations will be incredibly different. So, it's your job as the author to make it clear what the thoughts and feelings behind the actions are. That will help your readers get to know what kind of person your character is, so they can identify more closely with them.

Yes, there are times when not revealing motivations, especially those of the antagonist, builds useful suspense, so help yourself to those. But even if you're not showing your hand to the reader, you might want to know what cards you're holding. If you know the type, once the character's true motives are revealed, their previous actions will naturally align and make sense for readers.

So, starting out, try not to let yourself get overwhelmed with all the details of the type and trying to pack them into the story. Instead, ask yourself what major decisions your protagonist is making and whether you're being clear about why they're making them. Make sure their *why* aligns with the type's core motivations.

PROTAGONIST AND THEME

Once you feel comfortable working with your protagonist's type, a next step to building sound story framework is to find a theme that resonates strongly with the protagonist. I've included a list of those for each type in the previous section, and while it's by no means exhaustive, authors who are new to working with the Enneagram could do themselves a solid by picking one that's listed and going from there.

These themes are ones that the type will naturally do battle with over the course of their life as a result of their core motivations and the resulting attentional patterns. A Six is going to think a lot about the theme of loyalty, for instance. Starting out in their character arc, they're probably going to have some subconscious yet firm beliefs about loyalty. Loyalty is crucial to them and their core motivations. That means there's a lot for you, the author, to poke at there. It's likely to be a fruitful exploration because your character will probably have some triggers around loyalty and disloyalty, and as authors, we love knowing how to trigger our characters.

There's little more frustrating than jabbing at a character but the damn thing won't budge. When this happens, it means there's a part of us that know this character isn't motivated by the trigger we're providing. Now you know why it's happening, though, and you can adjust as needed. This is why it's a huge gift to our stories to pair a strong theme with the particular type.

An iconic character with no strong reactions of any kind is hardly iconic at all.

So go ahead and pair your Eight with a theme of injustice, say. Pair your Two with a theme of responsibility. Pair your Four with a theme of identity. Pair your Seven with a theme of freedom. There's no reason to try to reach too far here for something that's never been done, because if it's an effective and strong pair, it's been done. But it can still be done in a *new* way by you. I know that sounds clichéd, but it's true. It's in the combination of the innately familiar and something fresh that we create iconic characters. And only by triggering our iconic characters dramatically and effectively can we craft iconic stories.

IT'S NOT ALL OR NOTHING

When we feel like we're not up to the task of a new skill, we may feel anxiety about using it. If you've ever learned a new language, you'll understand what I mean. Anxiety does this thing in our brain where it shuts down nuanced thinking and puts us into all-or-nothing mode. If I can't speak Spanish perfectly, then I might as well stick with English while I'm in Mexico and see if they pick up on what I'm saying—that sort of thing.

I've heard the Enneagram described as a language model of psychology, but I assure you that you don't need to speak in full sentences before you can try it out.

If you notice yourself feeling like, "I'll never get this right," and you want to wait until you're a master of the types before you start using them, I've got bad news for you: that's not how it works.

There is knowledge and understanding that can only be gained through practice and experience, so waiting until you're an expert means you'll never begin.

The great thing is that even a little bit of application can go a long way. You can hold the type in your mind in the form of a character of a person you know of that type and use them as a basic avatar as you write. That's a great start. It's also how you get more fluent in your understanding and use.

I like to think of Enneagram application to storytelling as all a bonus. You're not being graded on a scale of 1 to 100; it's all extra credit. You may already be a strong writer, in which case, understanding your characters on this deeper level will simply turn you into a superstar.

If you notice the impulse to wait until you feel some sort of mastery on these concepts before you begin using them, I'll encourage you once again to pause and notice that this is likely all-or-nothing thinking born from anxiety. Maybe you think you'll look or feel stupid, maybe you're worried you'll mess things up, or maybe you just don't like the vulnerable feeling of being a beginner at something. Whatever the case, you don't have to listen to that anxiety, because there's actually nothing to be anxious about. You're in control here.

The first draft may feel like the gladiator arena where all your core fear and insecurities charge out of trapdoors with sharp weapons, but when you take a step back, you might find that the first draft is objectively a safe practice field. I like to tell people that what happens in the first draft is between you and your god. There is no lower-stakes environment available to the writer to practice facing your fears while also improving your craft.

If you experience a lot of anxiety around getting started on your draft (this can take the form of inexplicable procrastination, being easily distracted, feeling like you need to know more before starting without knowing precisely what it is you need to know, or a slew of other things parading as common sense), I suggest you check out my book *Sustain Your Author Career*.

However, sometimes simply noticing that we've slipped into all-or-nothing thinking can snap us out of it.

Don't expect to know how your first time using the Enneagram in your character development will go prior to trying it out. Form a hypothesis, sure, but you have to run the experiment and gather the data before you can draw a sound conclusion.

EXPLORE YOUR ENNEAGRAM TYPE

This is a big, big part of learning to write an iconic character, and that is: learn which type *you* are so you don't blend yourself with types that aren't that.

This is, by far, the most common issue authors run into when first writing with the Enneagram. Because they haven't identified their own core fear and desire and begun to unpack how it leads to their patterns of thinking, feeling, and behaving in daily life, they will inject their fear or desire into characters where it doesn't belong. On a subconscious level, the author is asking, "What would I do in this scenario?" or "What decision would I make?" rather than taking a step back and asking what the character would be motivated to do based on their type. Readers pick up on this inconsistency, even if they can't name what's happening.

Sometimes this happens on a book-level scale. An author who is a cerebral Five but hasn't identified that and begun to "see" the lens they use might only write logically minded characters. They may have such a disdain for large displays of emotions or letting the heart decide that none of the characters (except, perhaps, the villains) act in that way. Instead, the Five is subconsciously projecting what they would do in each situation, for each conflict, and having the characters act similarly. The result is that all of the characters sound a little bit the same and the story feels flat, with none of the characters jumping off the page.

Or perhaps an author is a strong and bold Eight and hasn't identified their own distaste for hesitation, pausing to feel emotions, and letting things go. In this case, they might struggle to keep interpersonal conflict going throughout the story because every character knows exactly what they want and runs through walls to get it as soon as possible. The characters don't sit and stew on their feelings or withdraw to process because the author doesn't have experience with those options and doesn't even see them as tolerable routes for conflict.

There is a massive shift in our awareness when we first realize that we've been seeing the world through a particular and limited lens, one different from most everyone else we encounter. We like to believe that we're getting an objective view of reality, so it's disarming to consider that we're not even close to it, and that another person's vastly different perspective might be just as valid and valuable as our own.

This is the seismic shift that happens when we start doing our own Enneagram work as authors, and until we experience the massive implications of that, our ability to create these different types in our work without constantly overlaying our own type onto them will be greatly limited.

If you want to discover your own Enneagram type and learn how you might be unintentionally overlaying your lens onto all of your characters, I suggest the Integrative Enneagram's paid iEQ9 Questionnaire and a one-hour consultation with me to understand the results and begin uncovering where they're influencing your storytelling abilities and author career decisions. You can find those options at www.liberatedwriter.com.

RESOURCES FOR DEEPER READING

Let's say you're a Type 9, but you want to write an iconic character who is a Type 8. One of the techniques I suggest for developing an intuitive understanding of a type is to read the description of it from multiple sources. Different descriptions of the types will naturally be delivered in slightly different ways, with a focus on particular aspects and using language that may resonate more or less with you. You never know what sentence will jump off the page and be that final piece that brings the whole thing to life for you.

The descriptions I've included are filtered through my lens. I do a lot of work to keep the lens from being covered in Vaseline, but that doesn't mean I don't have a lens. So, read the descriptions I include in this book, but also don't be afraid to read the descriptions written by people with other lenses. This can help you see a type from multiple angles to develop a fuller picture.

Here are some free online resources I recommend:

The Enneagram Institute website:

www.enneagraminstitute.com

The Enneagram Spectrum of Personality Styles website:

www.enneagramspectrum.com

The Integrative Enneagram website:

www.integrative9.com

Some of you might want to go even deeper, and thankfully there are all kinds of books on the Enneagram you can dive into. They don't bring the storytelling element into the descriptions, but you, a storyteller, can certainly apply what you know about people to your characters without too much trouble.

You can browse some of my favorite Enneagram books (and more recommendations) here:

www.ffs.media/reading-recommendations

WHAT EACH OF US BRINGS TO THE PROCESS

One thing I especially love about the Enneagram is that there are no "shoulds" involved. It's a guide to help you make informed decisions with your characters, but it doesn't say that you *should* do anything. It offers interesting insight that you can play around with, if you so choose.

The major benefit I've found in using this framework for my own fiction, outside of writing objectively more coherent characters that some might even consider iconic, is that it's just damn good fun. It helps me approach writing as an exploration and a playground. It keeps me curious and engaged. It helps me feel connected to my characters, which makes the whole process more interesting and meaningful.

If you find that using this framework is not making your writing process easier, or that it's producing anxiety in you, that's important to notice. It doesn't mean that it's not right for you, but it might not be right for you *right now*, at least not until you can get to the bottom of why a tool like this is making the experience worse rather than better. You may discover some of your own patterns of thinking and feeling are calling out to be seen, unpacked, and deconstructed. That's one of those things that sometimes feels like a bummer but turns out to be a net positive on the other side of it.

What I expect will be the case for most of the folks reading this book, however, is that you'll fall back in love with your writing. Like a married couple that's drifted apart over the years, you can be brought back together with your characters through deeper understanding and appreciation. You'll experience the deep enjoyment of breakthrough discoveries, and those scenes that your gut told you needed to be there but your head couldn't make fit will suddenly slide into place. They may even have been the missing pieces to make your story a masterpiece.

While we may intuitively recognize each of the Enneagram types from our own lived experience, not to mention the fiction we've read throughout our lives, learning to put words to it, to be able to talk about each type, and to understand how motivation leads to thoughts, emotions, and behaviors is a crucial step to becoming master storytellers.

In each author, there's an altruistic impulse behind telling a story and wanting someone else to enjoy it. Exploring the Enneagram types supports that impulse.

And in each author, there's also a Machiavellian impulse to be the one pulling all the strings in the world of your making. Exploring the Enneagram types supports that impulse, as well.

My altruistic impulse in writing this book has always been to help authors stay connected to and in love with their writing as they gain new skills and continue to grow and improve their craft. I'm hoping I've accomplished that for at least a few of you.

My Machiavellian impulse in writing this book is... for me alone to know. But maybe by now you can guess that as a One whose core fear is being bad or corrupt, I've (mostly) kept your best interests at heart.

ABOUT CLAIRE TAYLOR

Claire Taylor is an independent author and the owner of FFS Media. She offers courses, coaching, and consulting for writers who want to supercharge their fiction and align their career using the Enneagram.

She still lives in her hometown of Austin, Texas.

Find her author services and fiction at liberatedwriter.com.

To receive tips and tricks to make your next story unforgettable, sign up for the Liberated Writer newsletter: liberatedwriter.com/join.

www.ingramcontent.com/pod-product-compliance
Lightning Source LLC
Chambersburg PA
CBHW022045020426
42335CB00012B/549